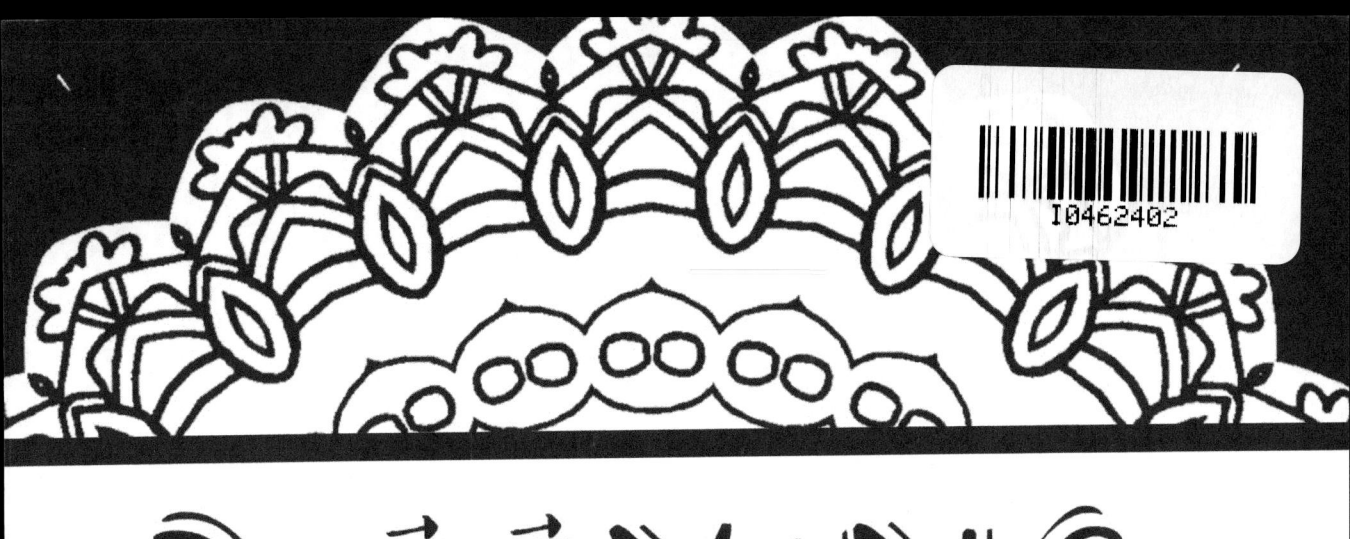

DIZZYING

DETAILS

#withmspdgtt #onecurioushuman

50 SINGLE SIDED PAGES FEATURING

EDGE TO EDGE PATTERNS AND MANDALAS!

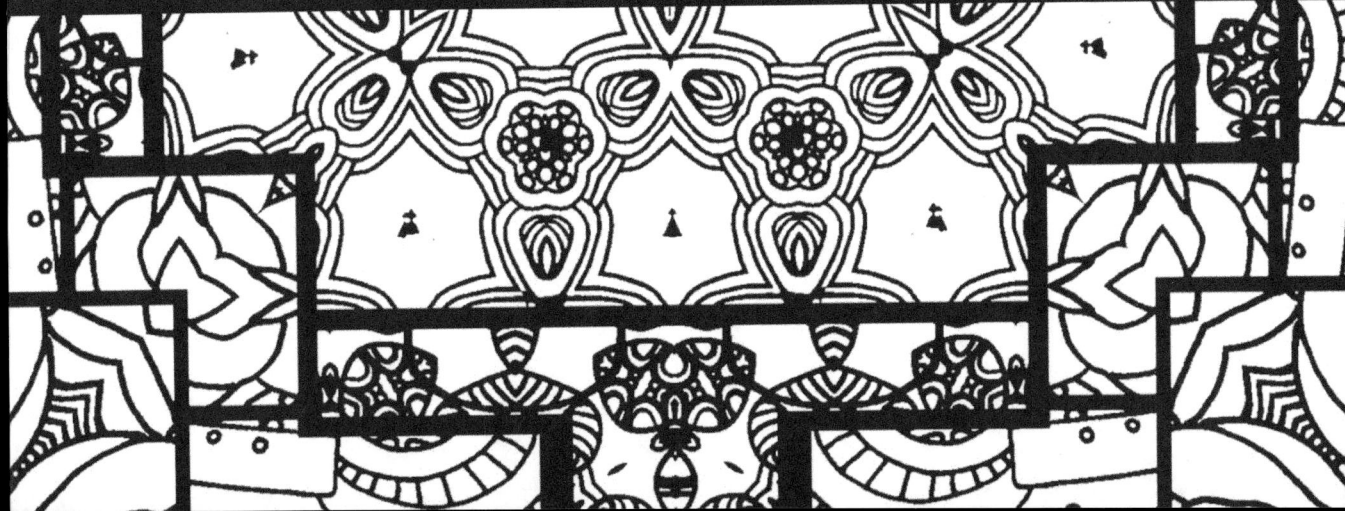

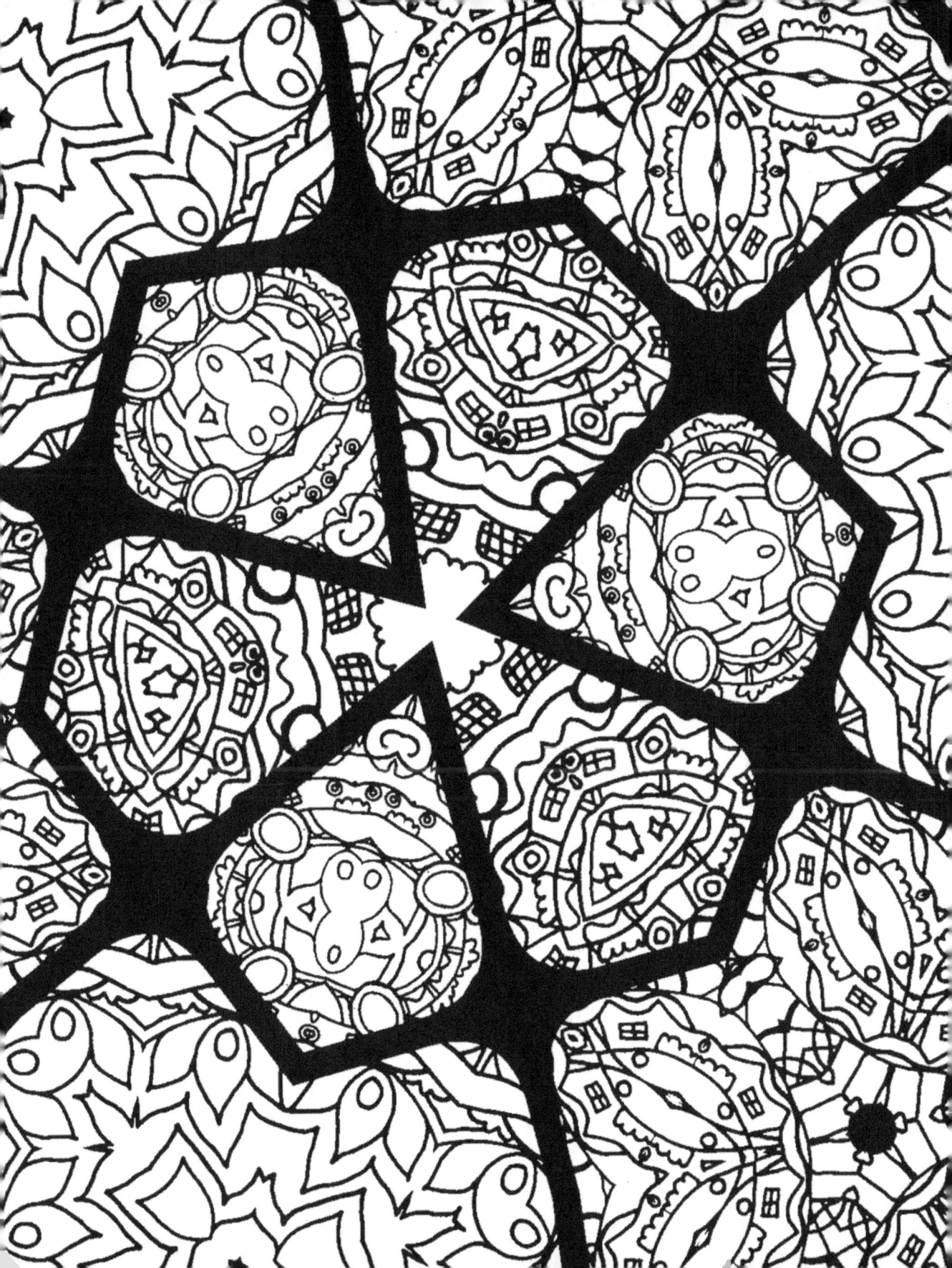

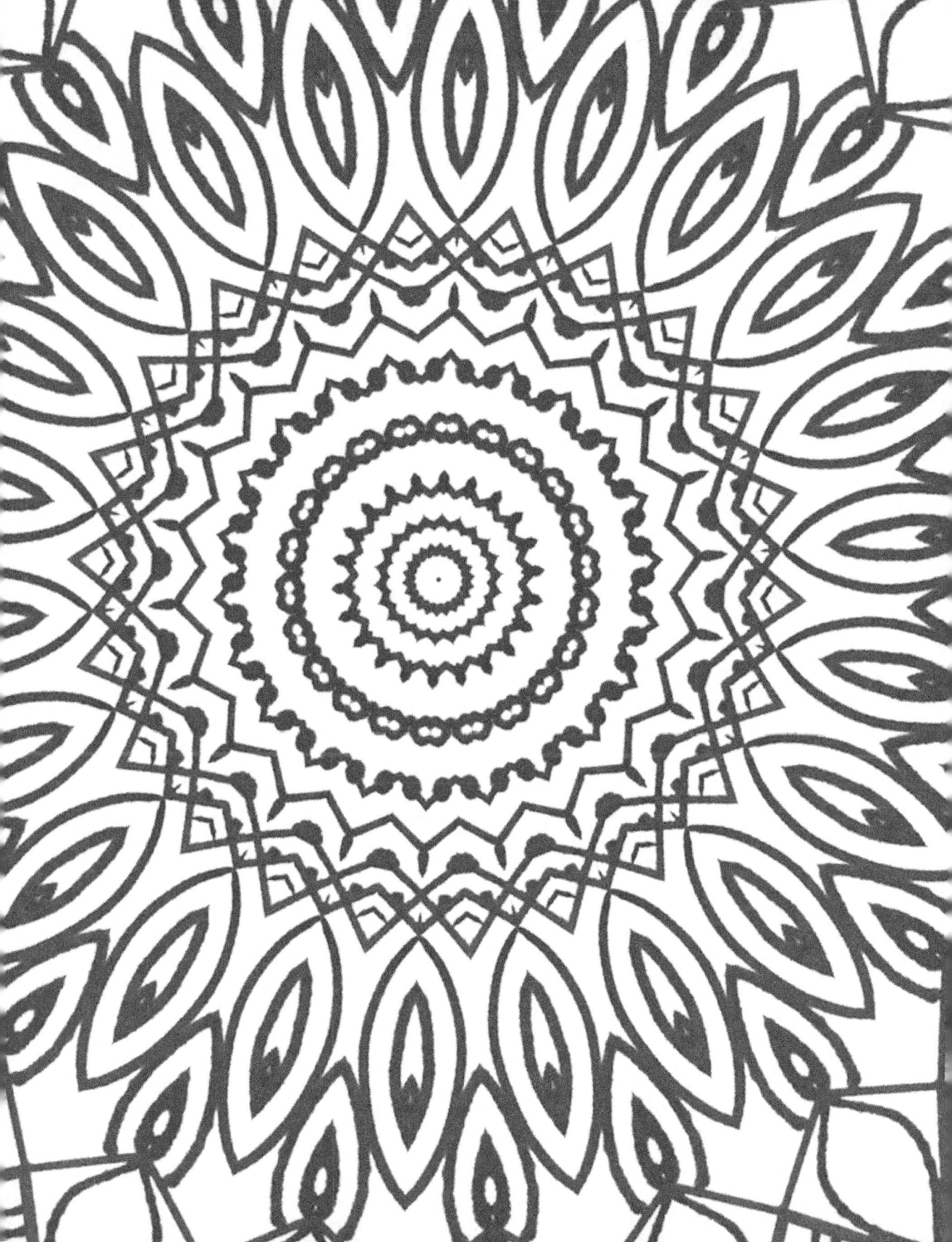

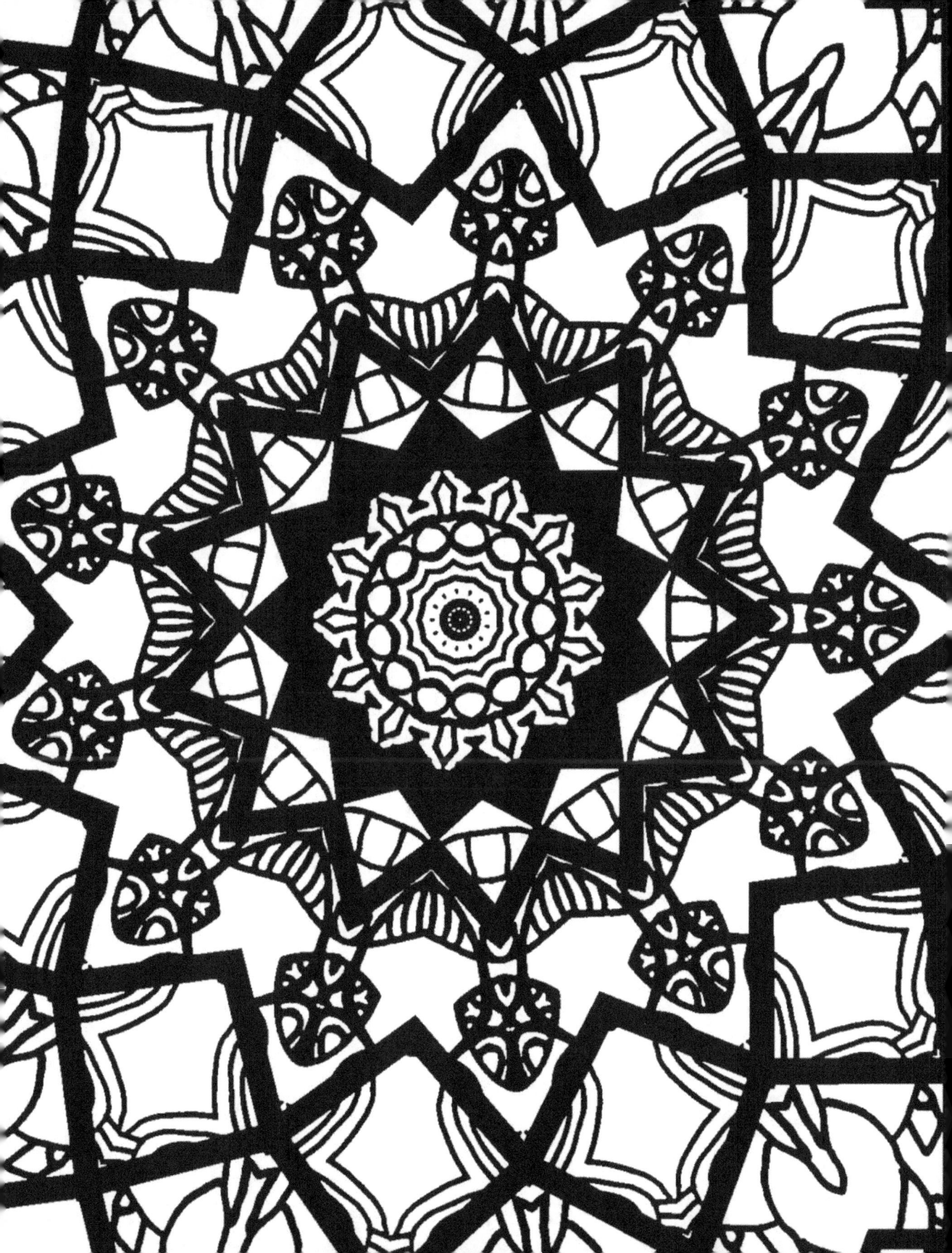

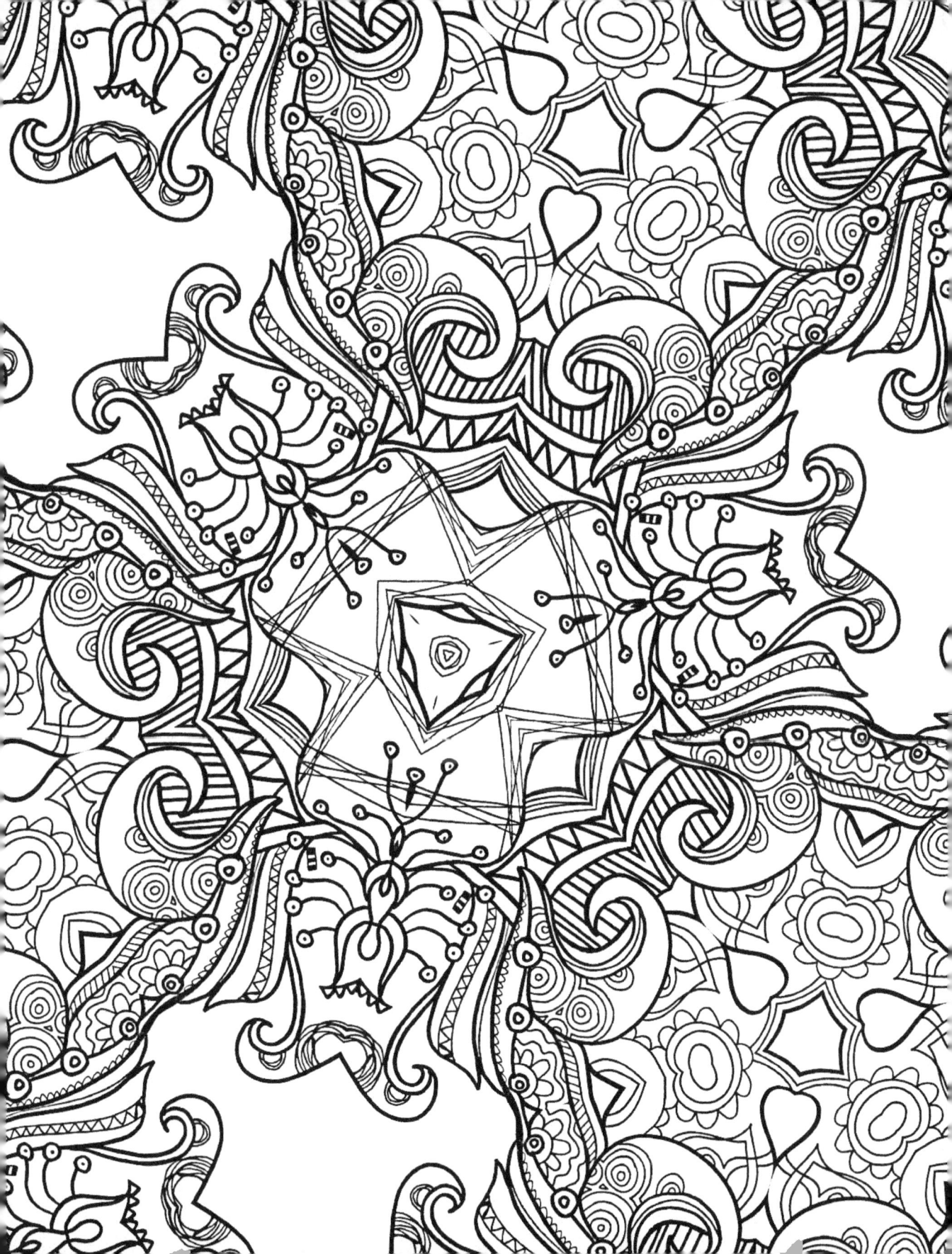

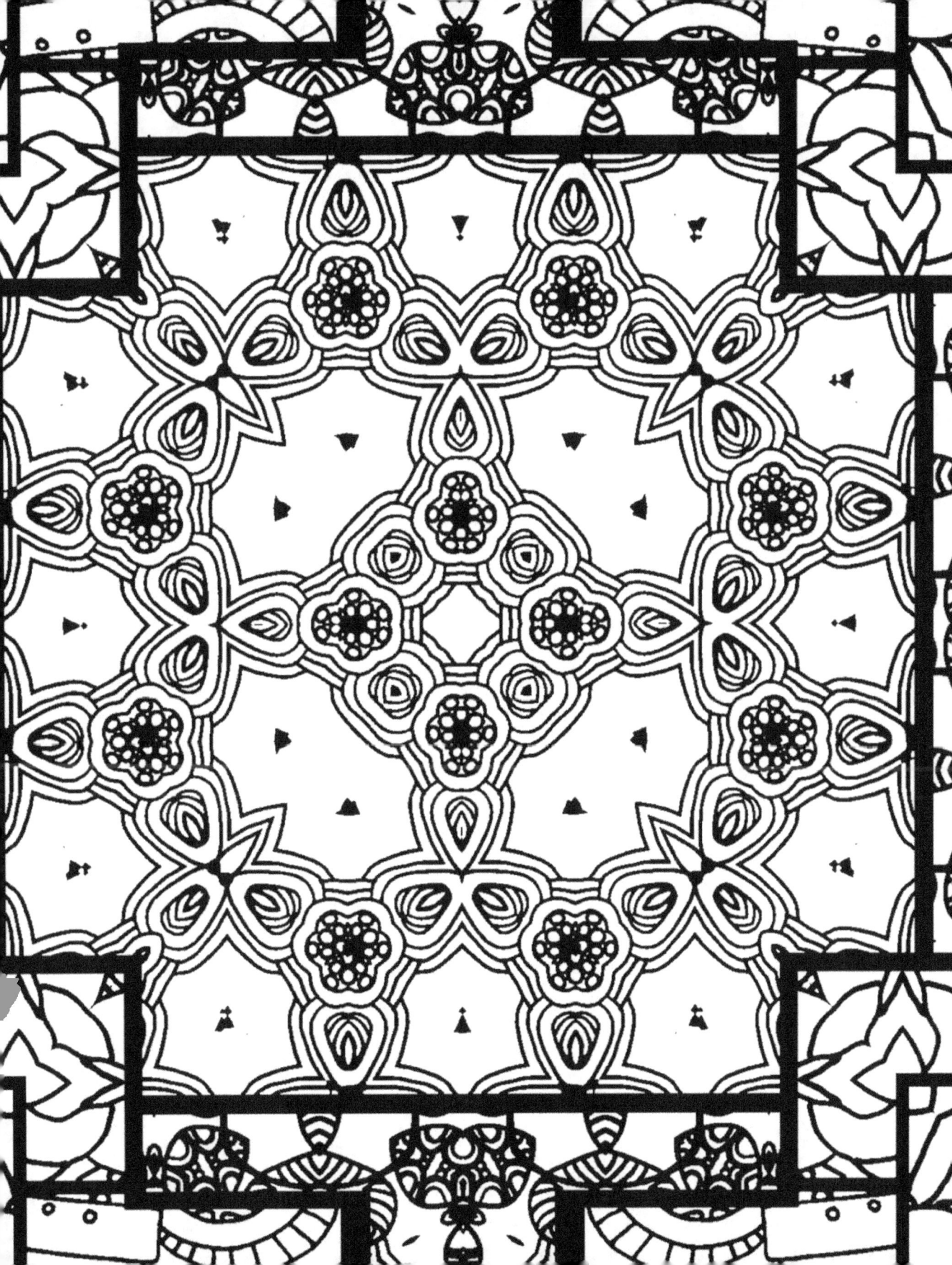

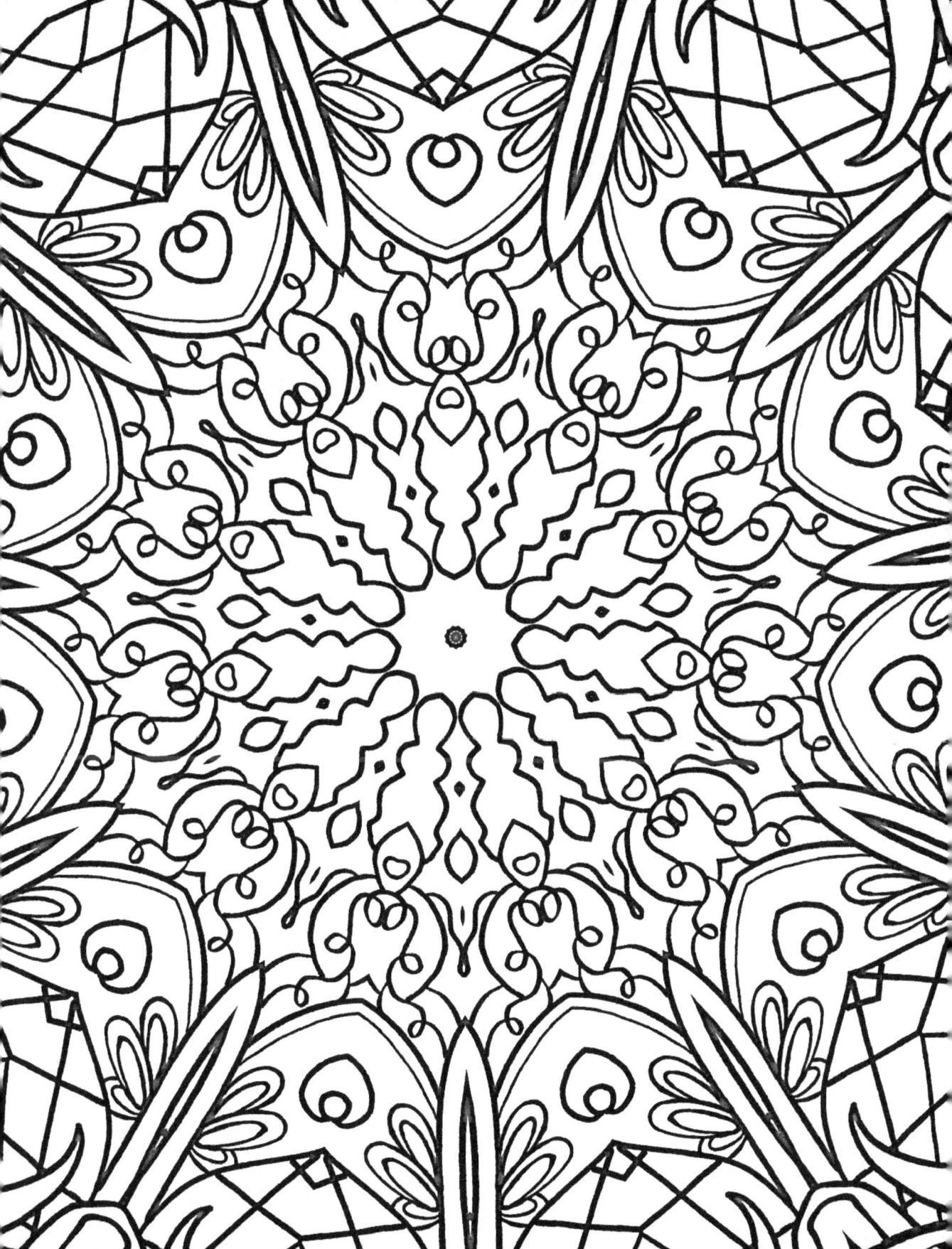

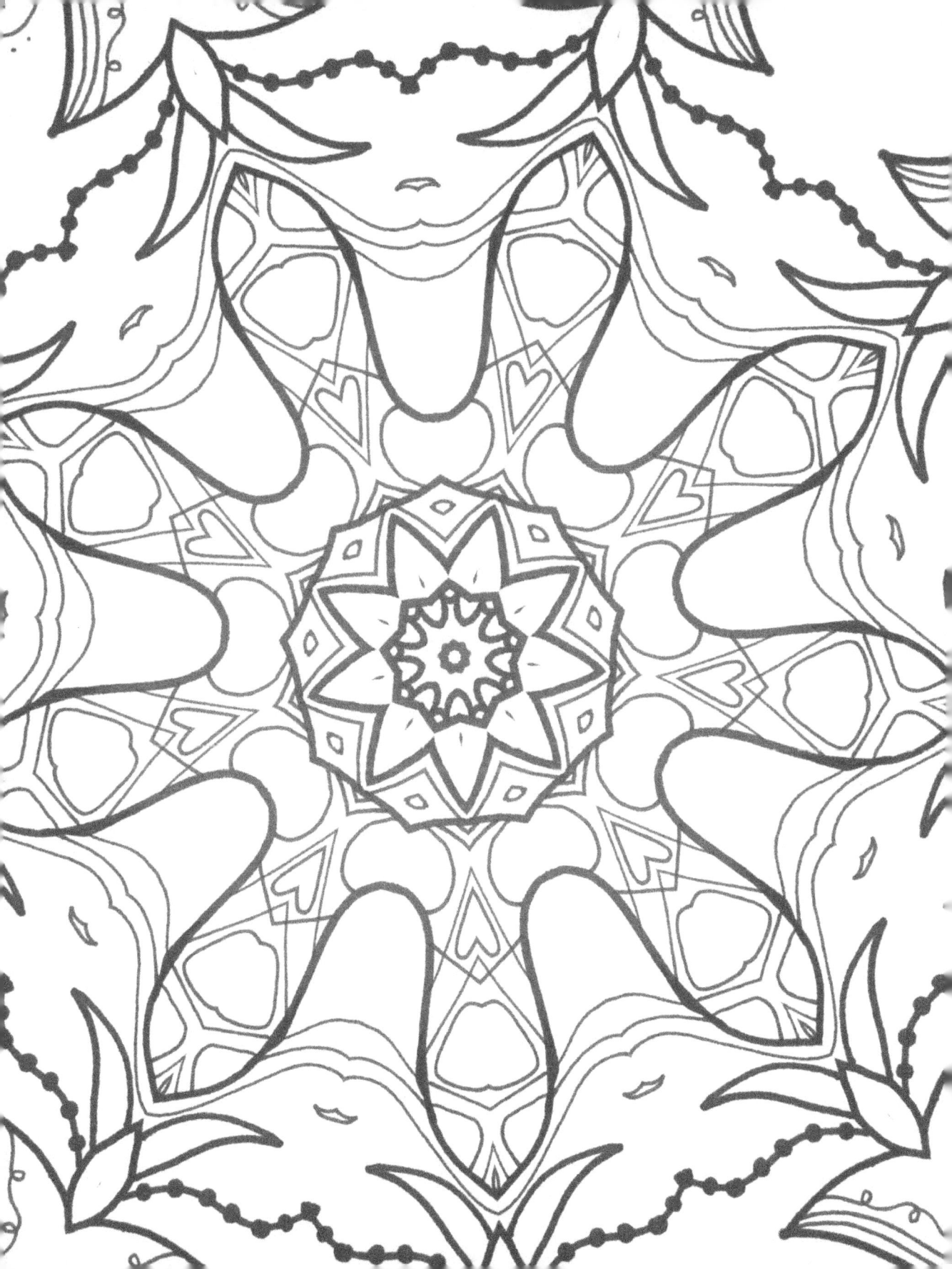

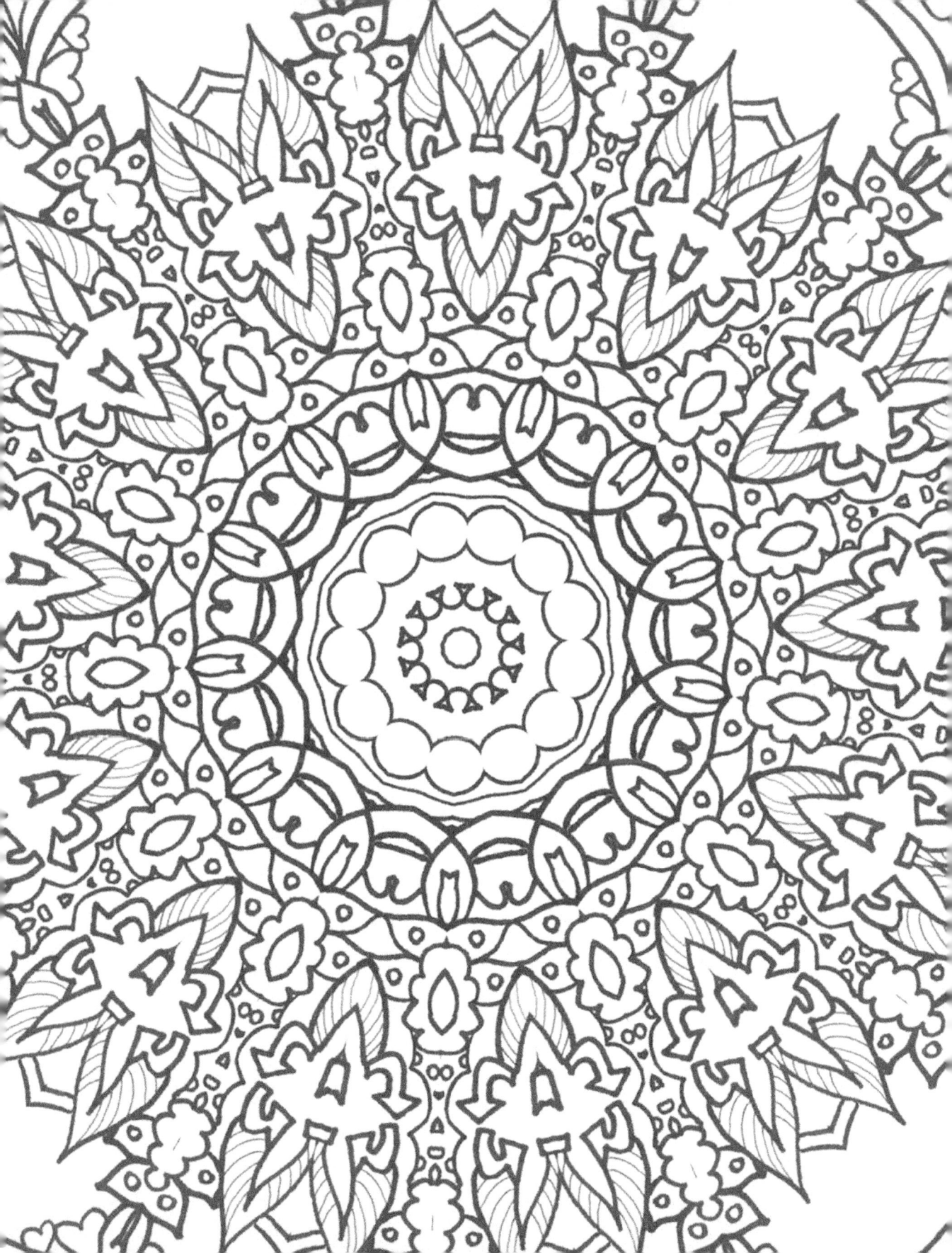

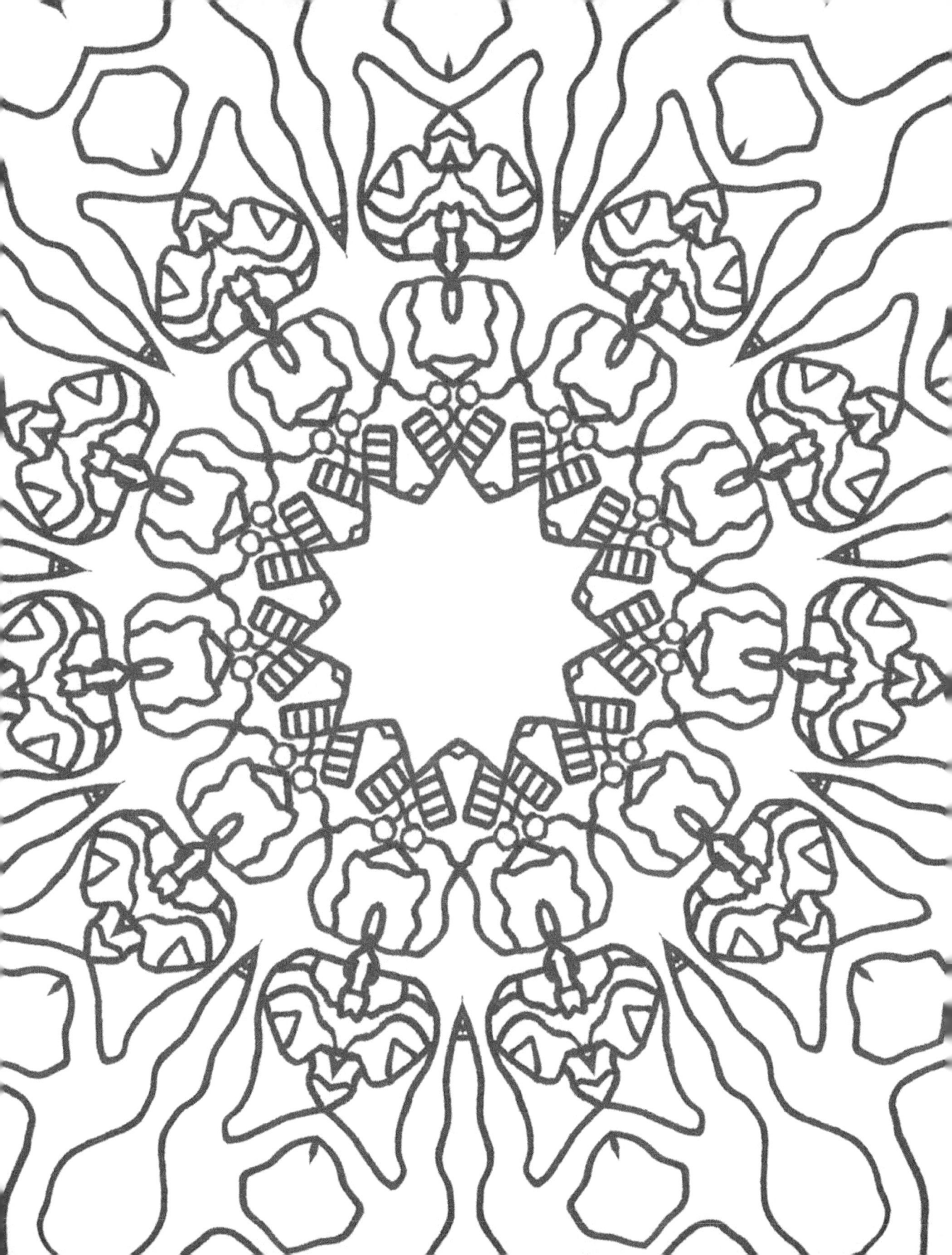

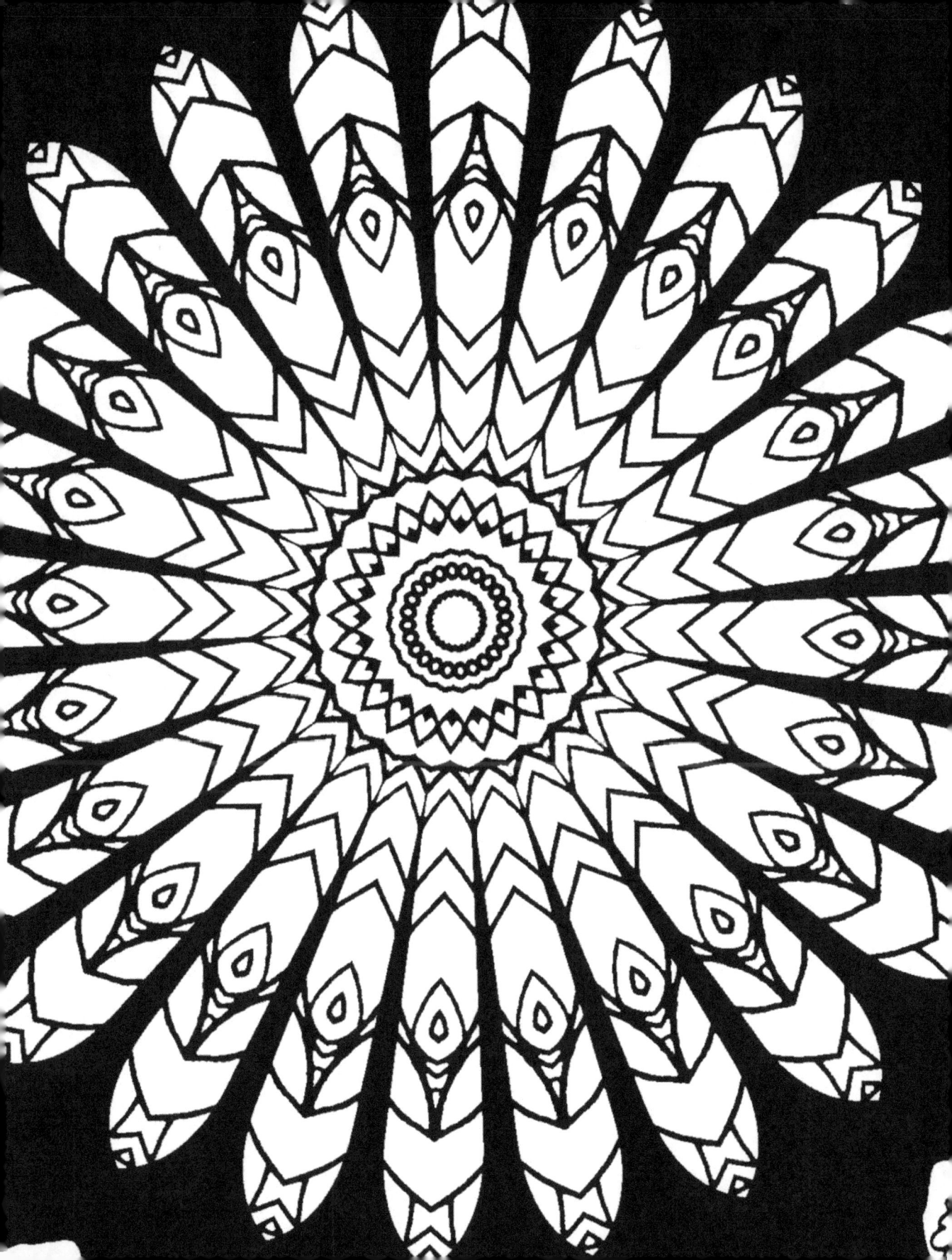

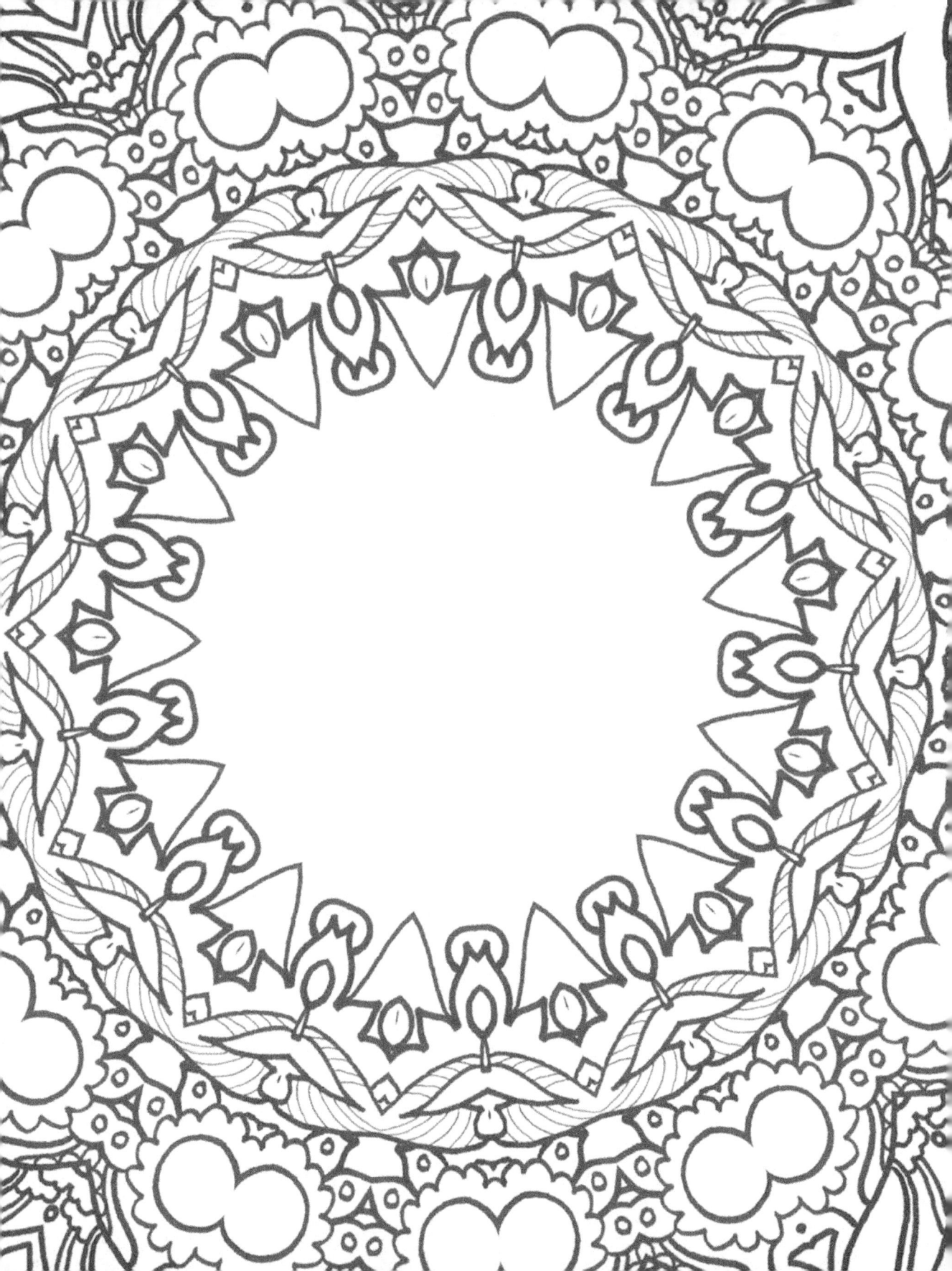

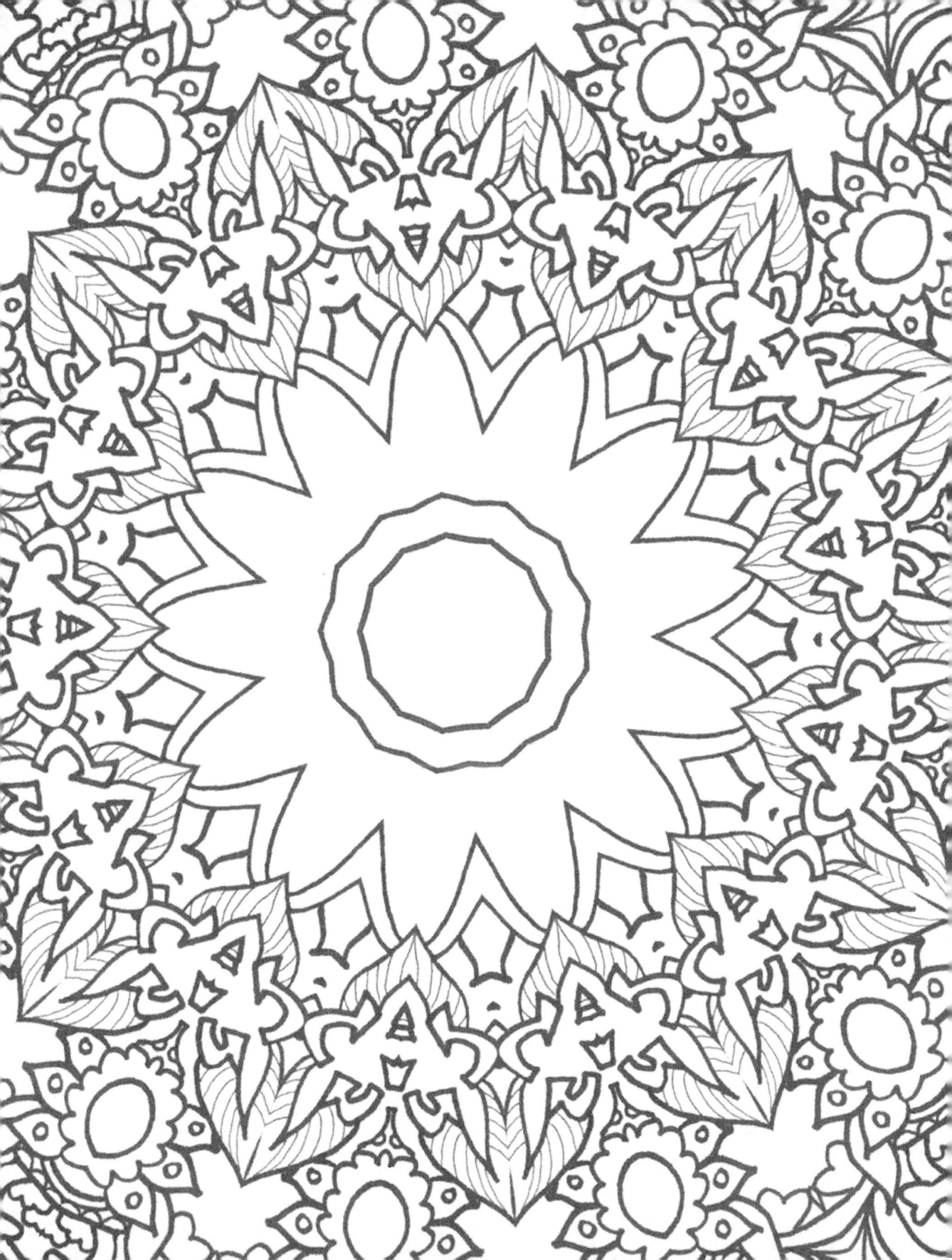

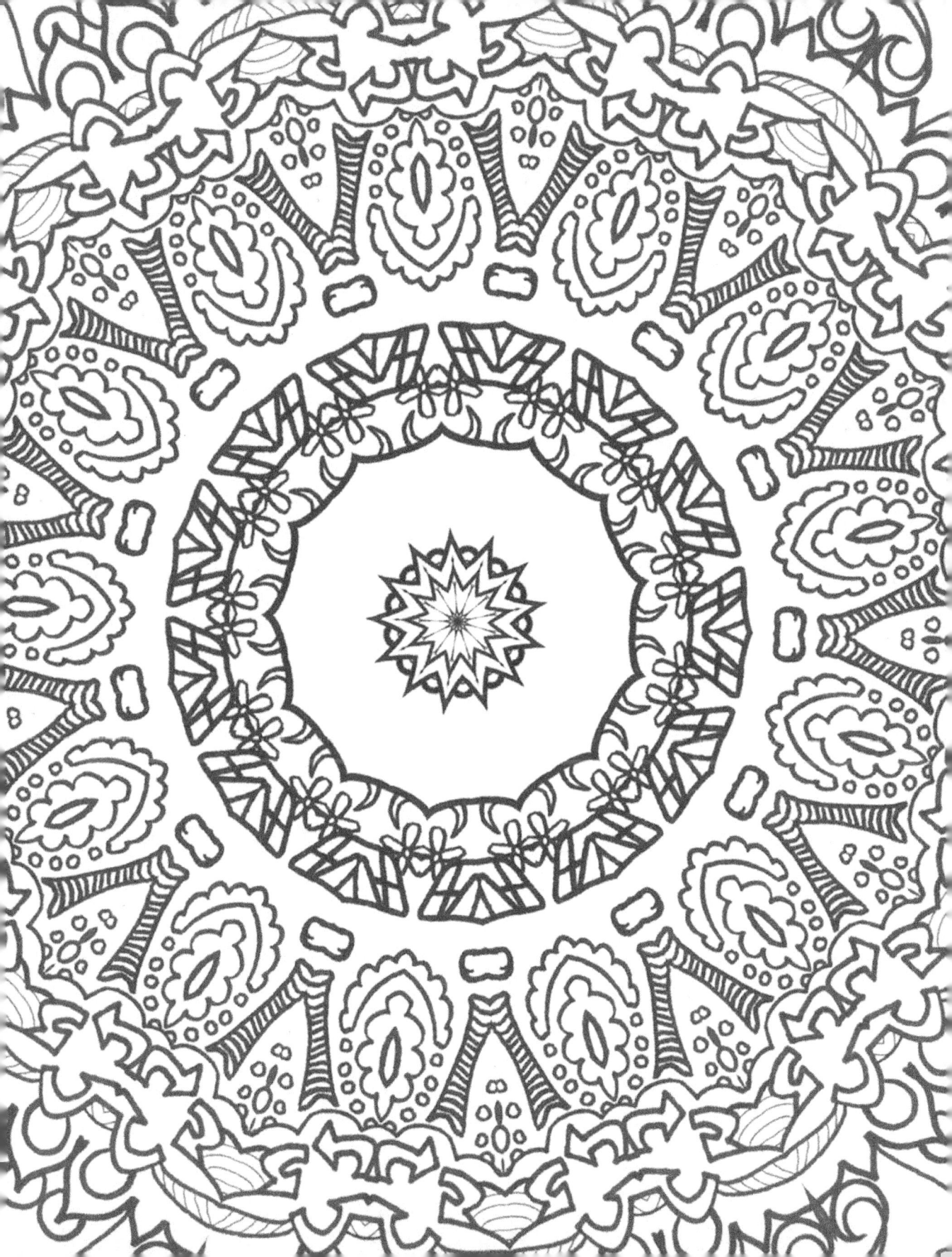

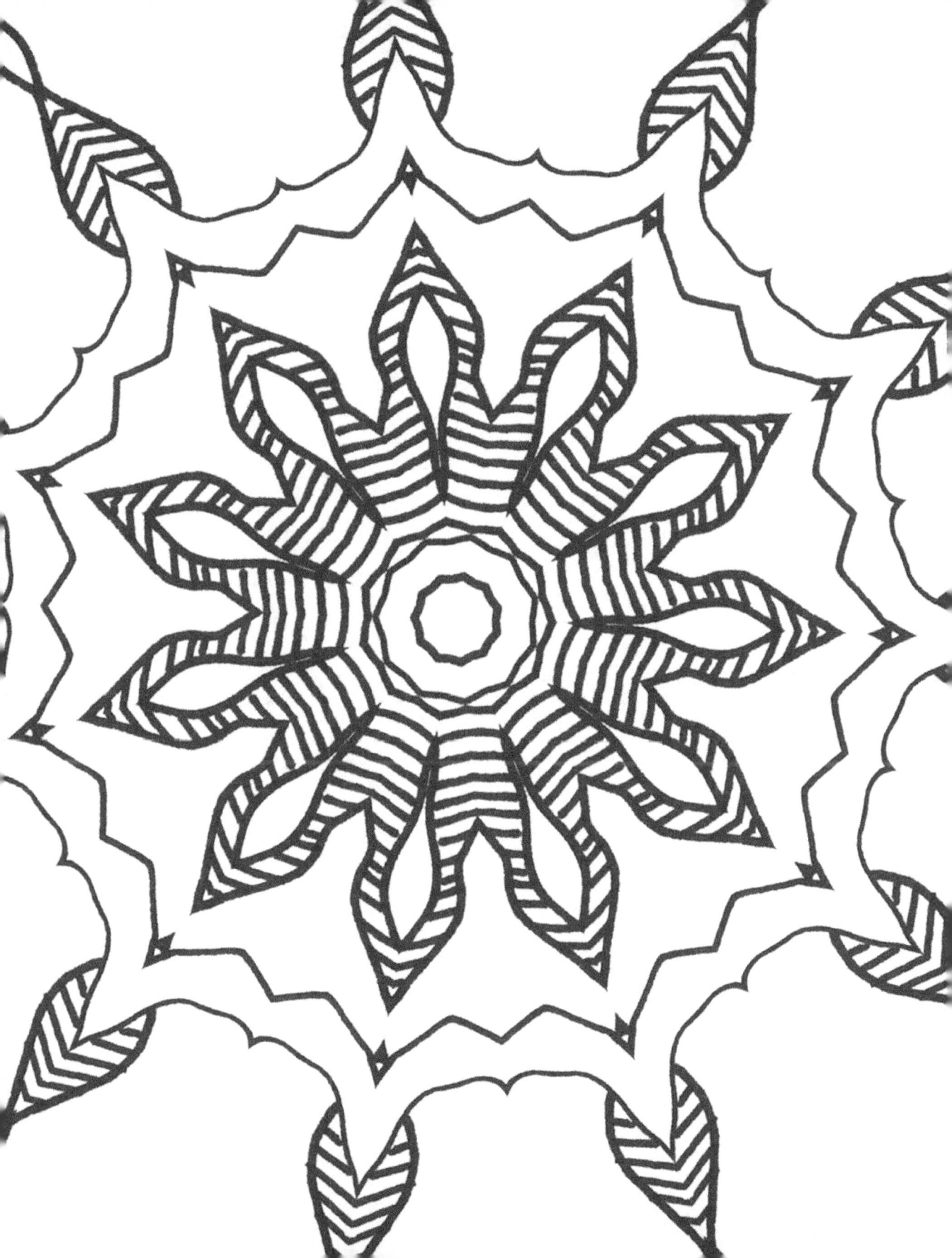

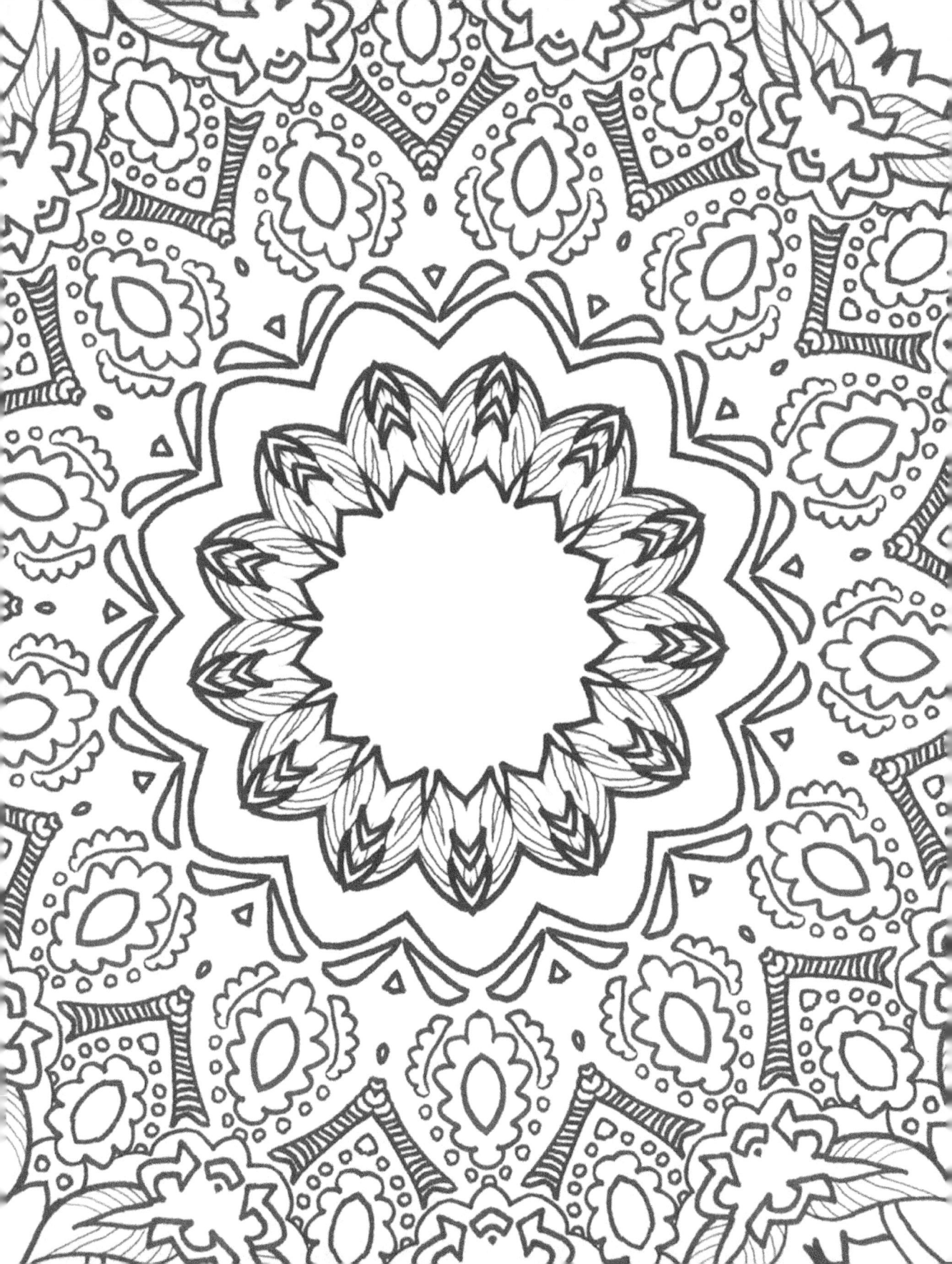

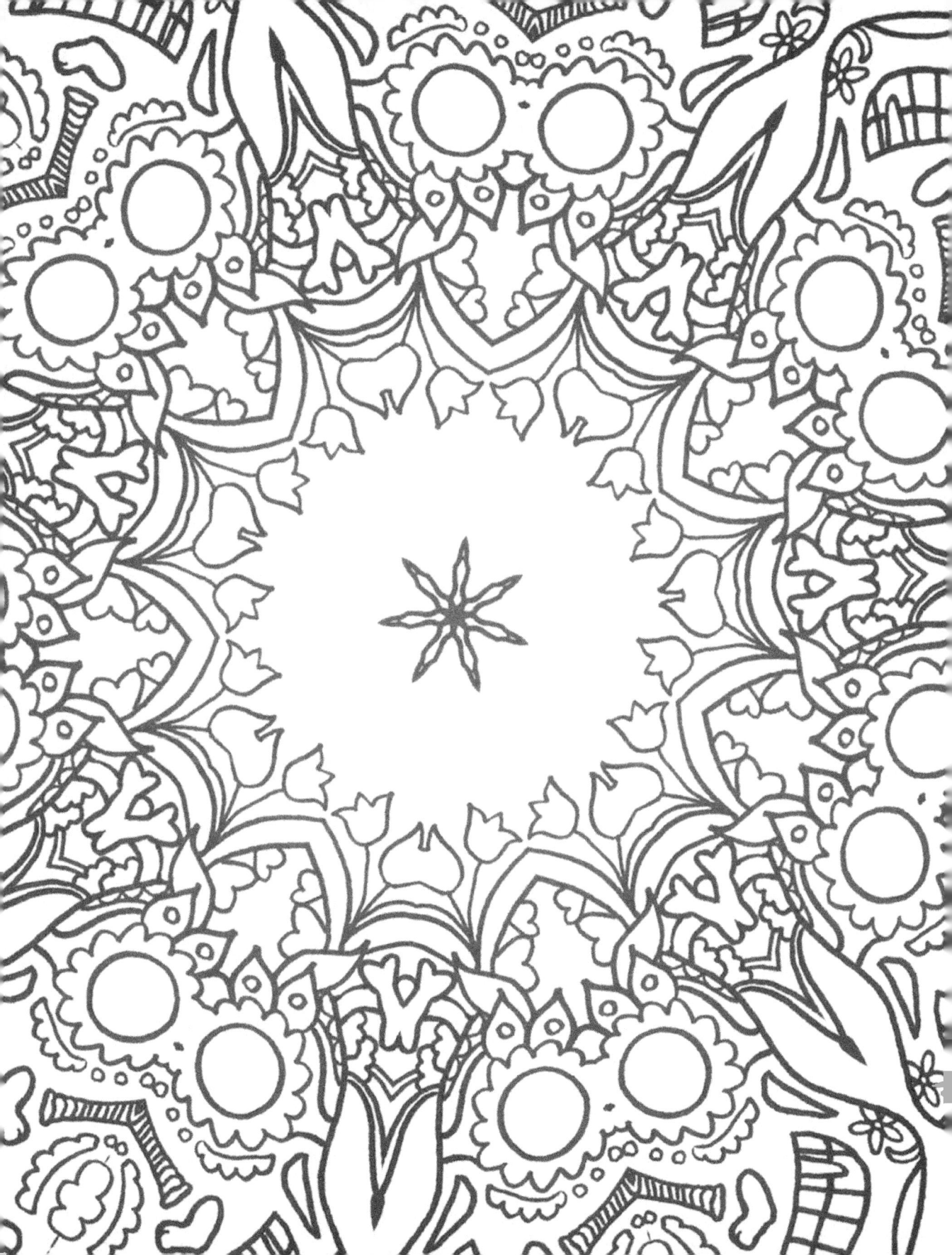

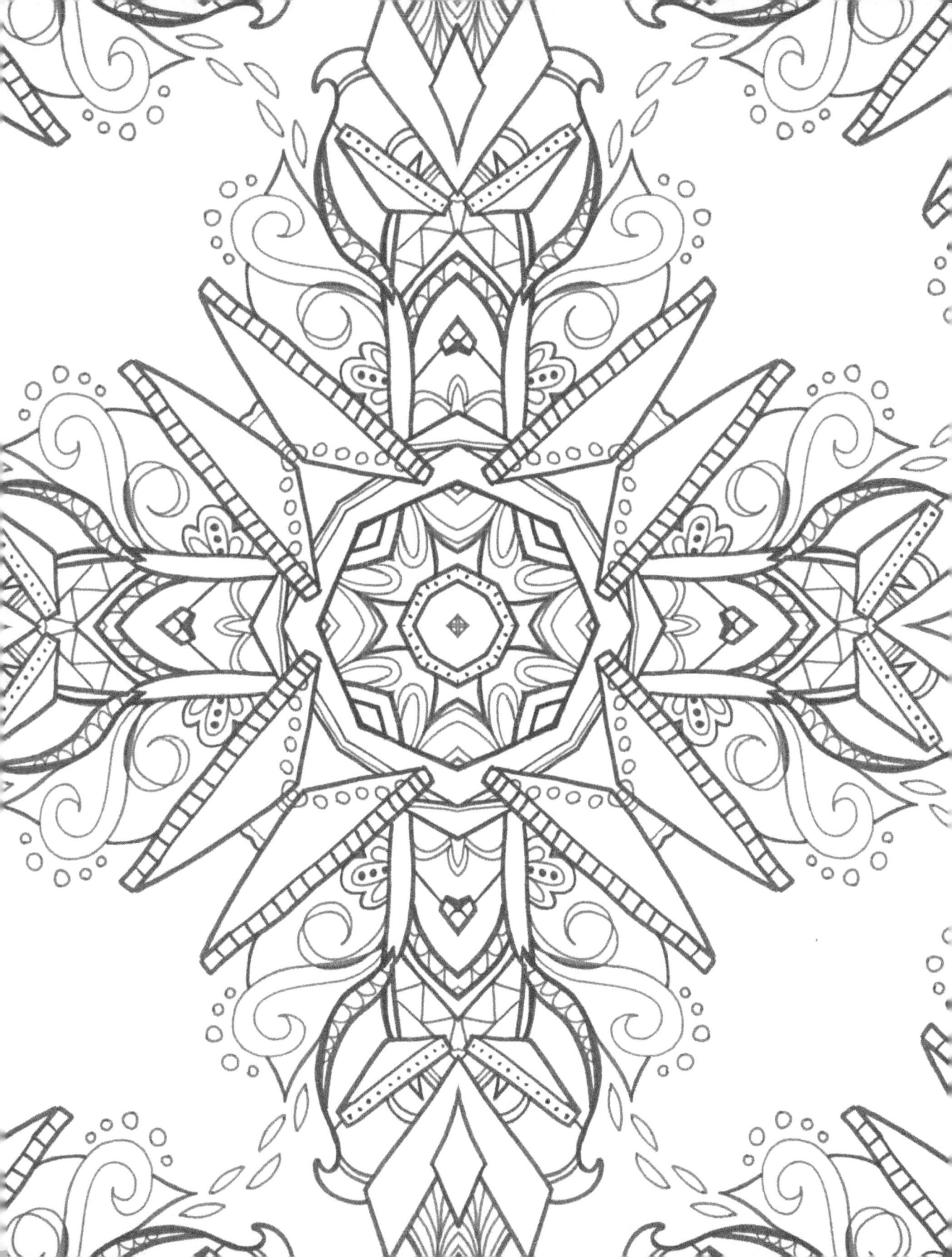

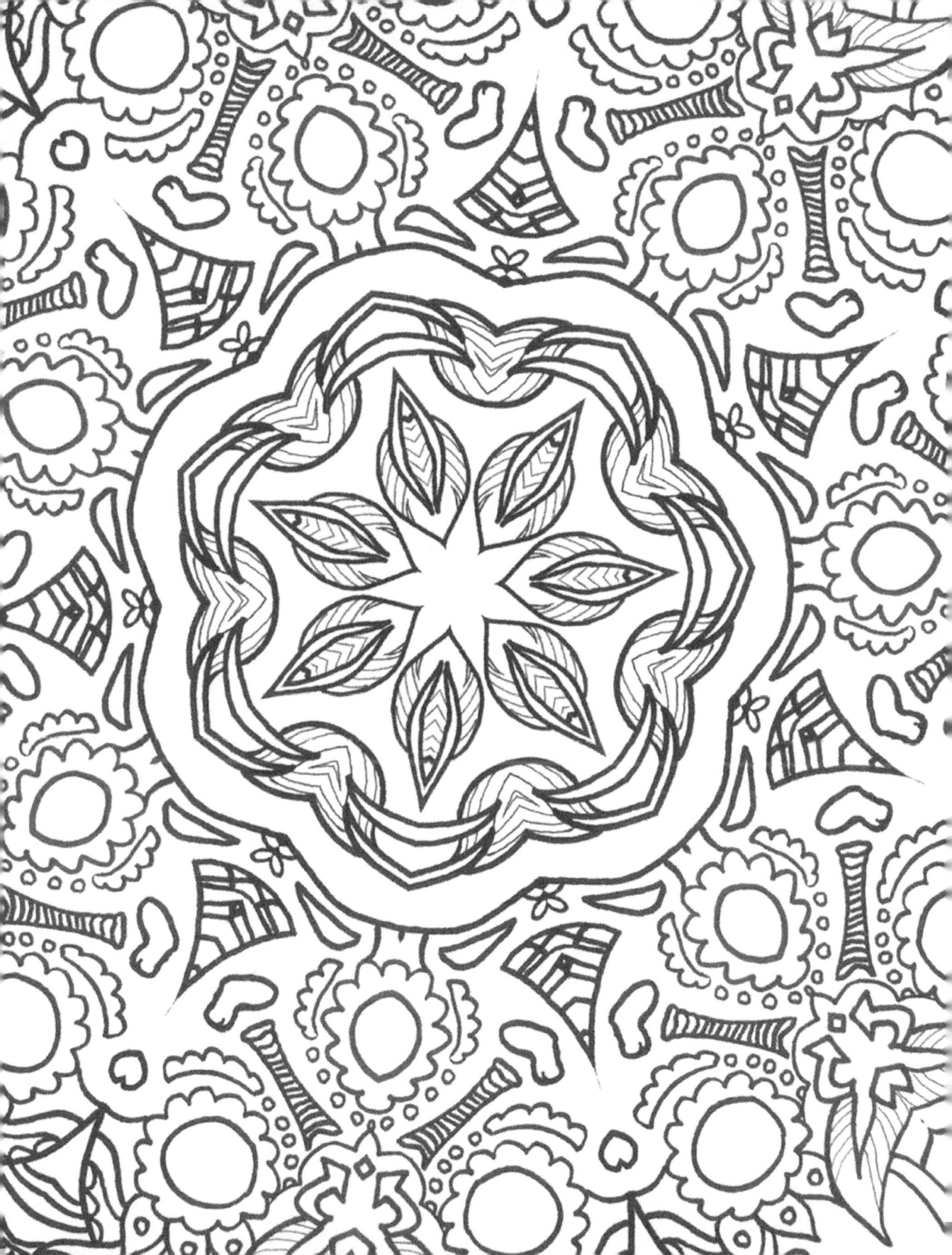

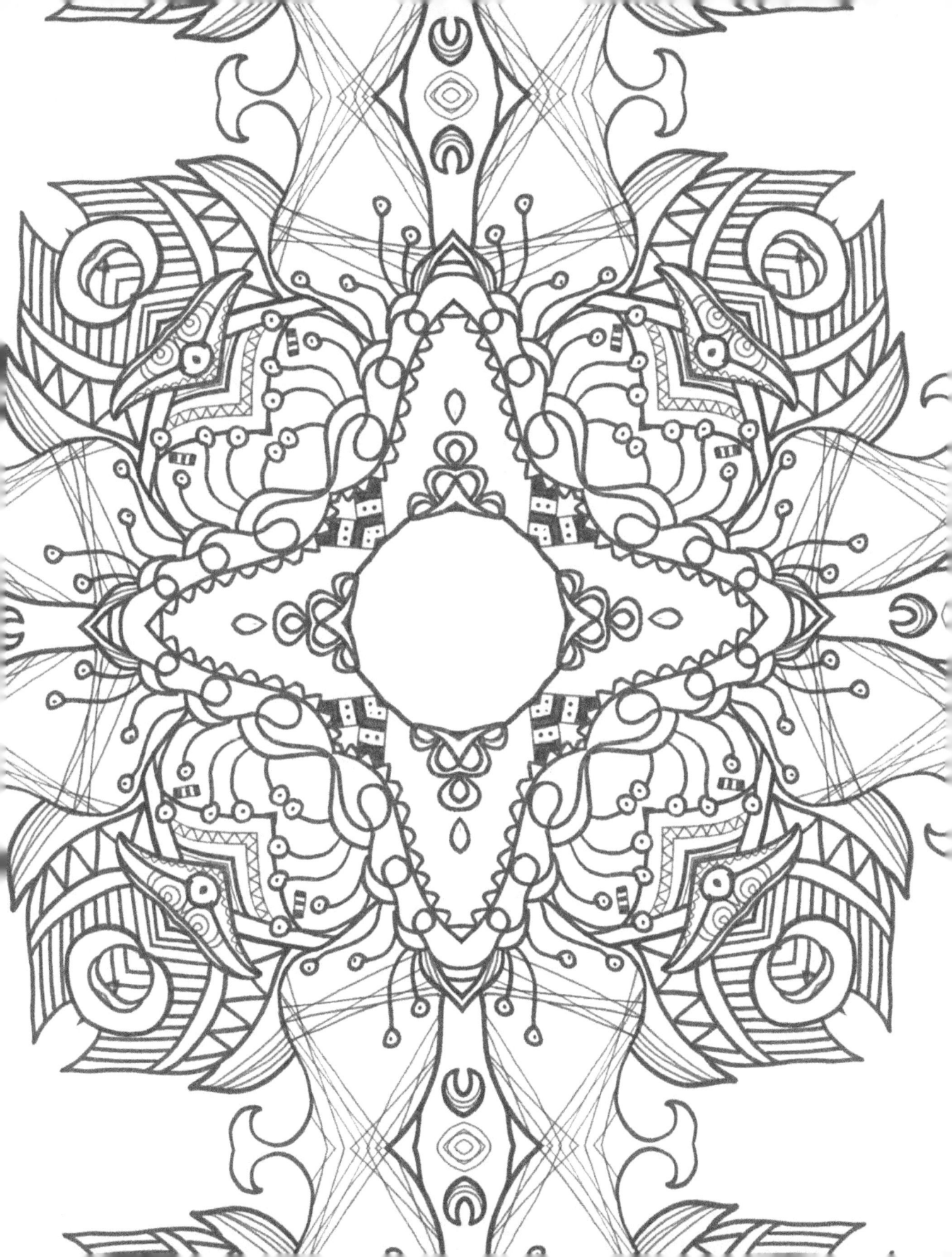

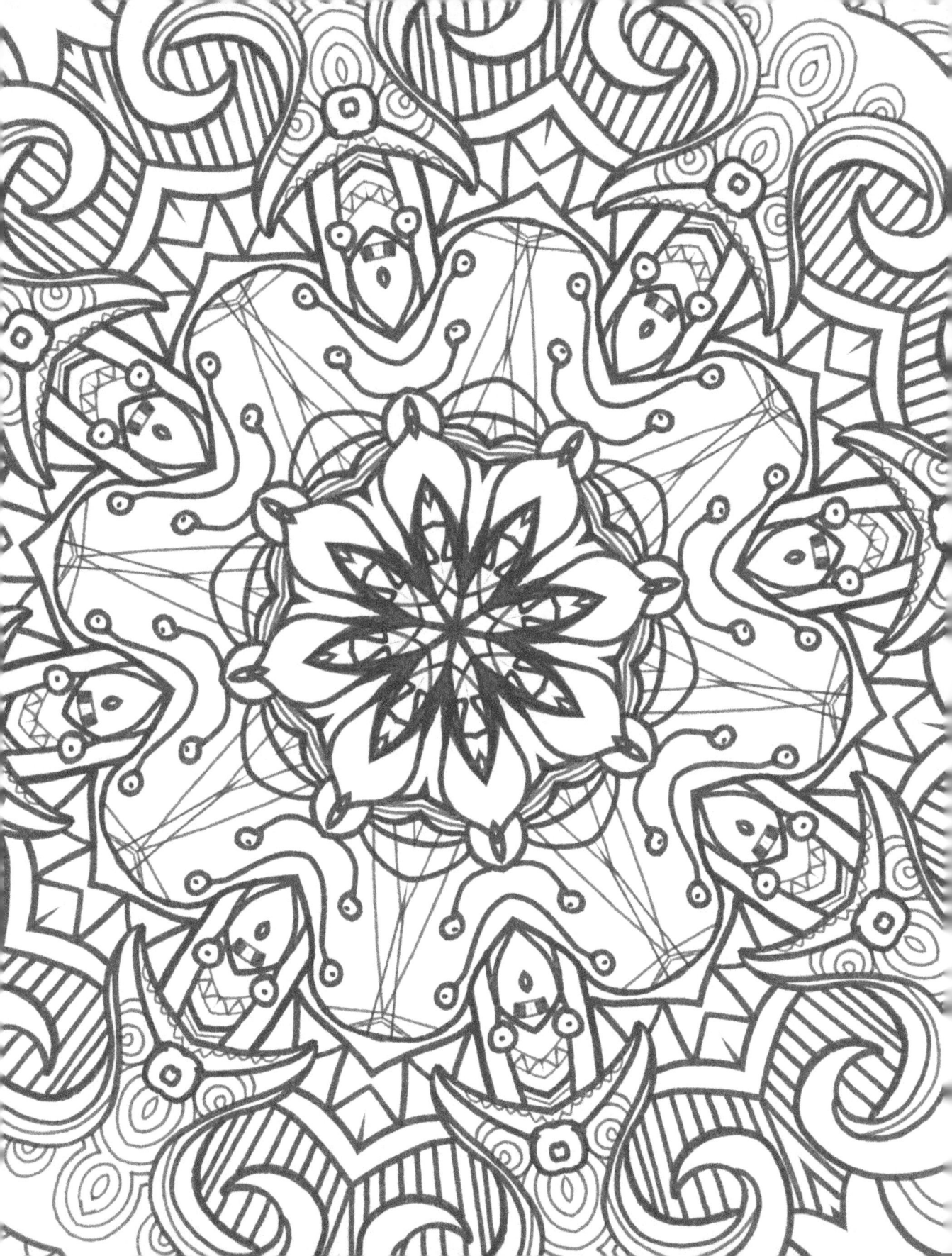

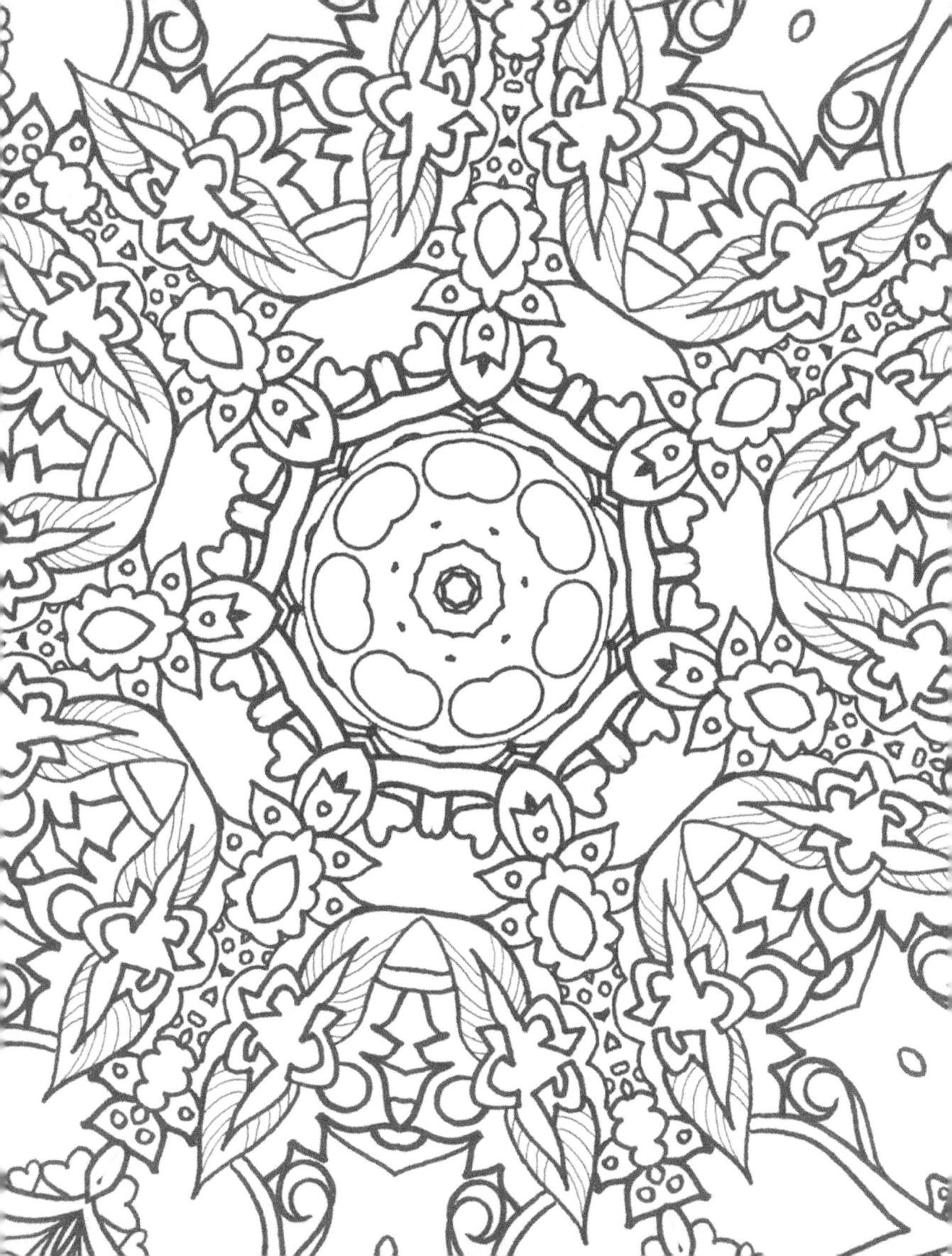

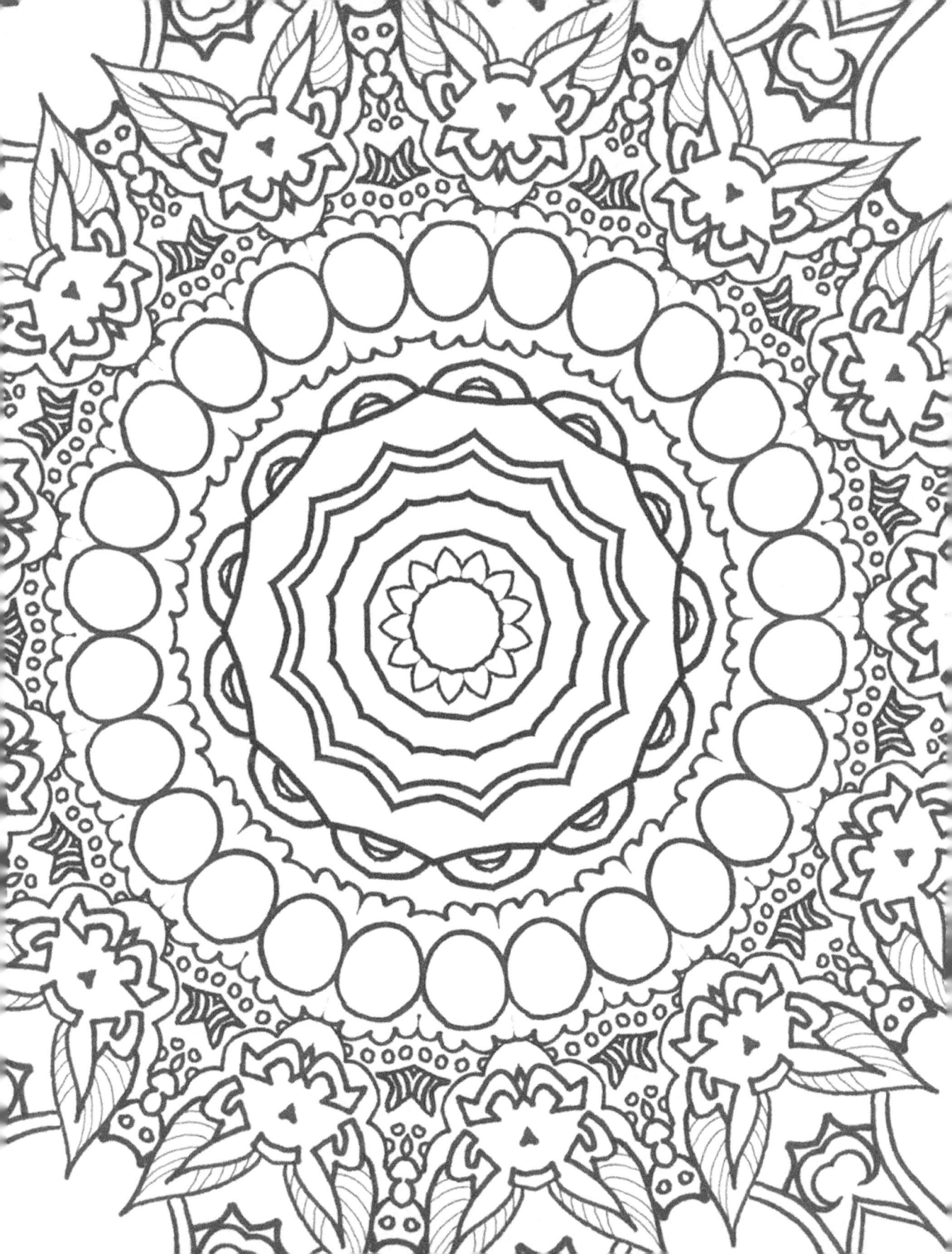

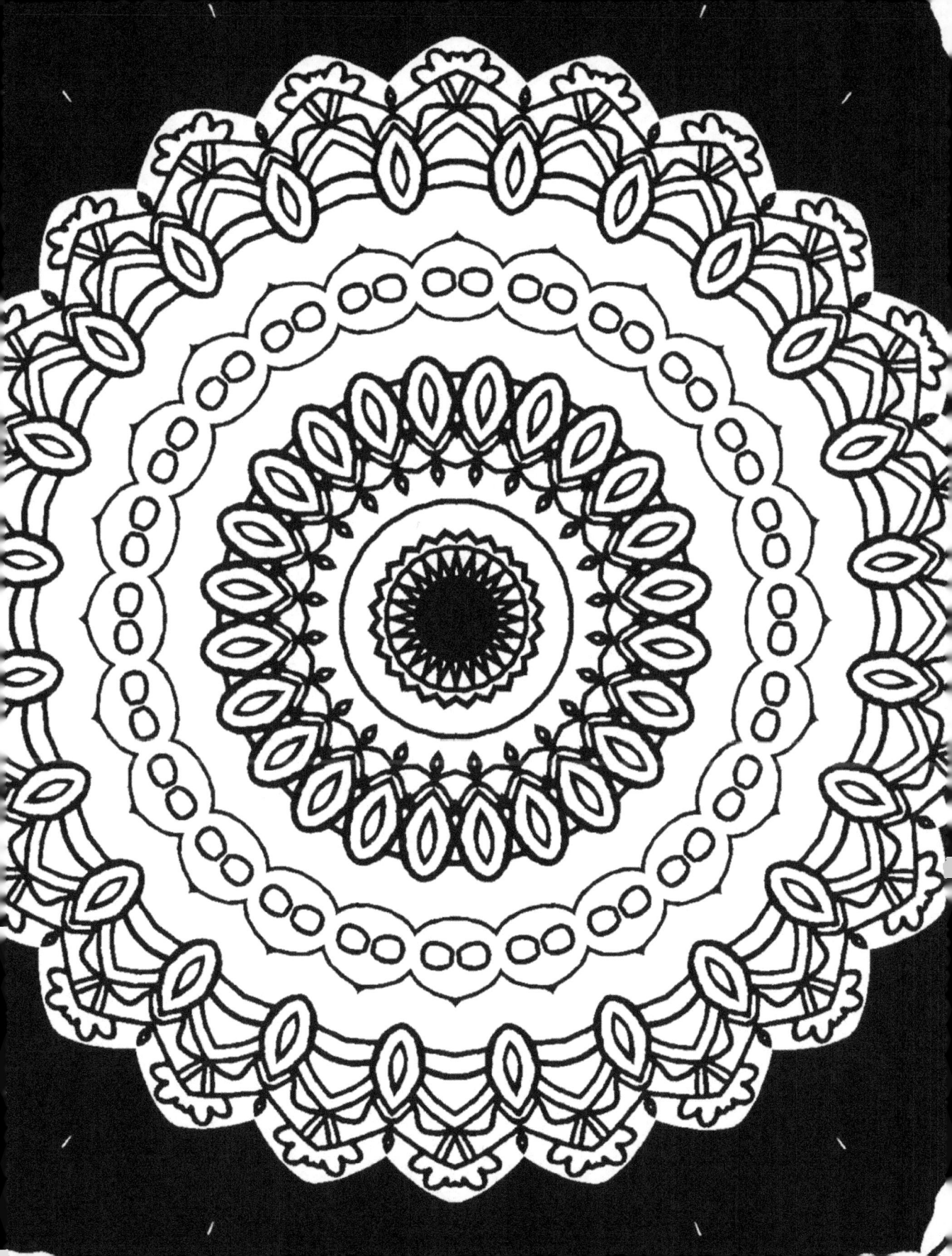

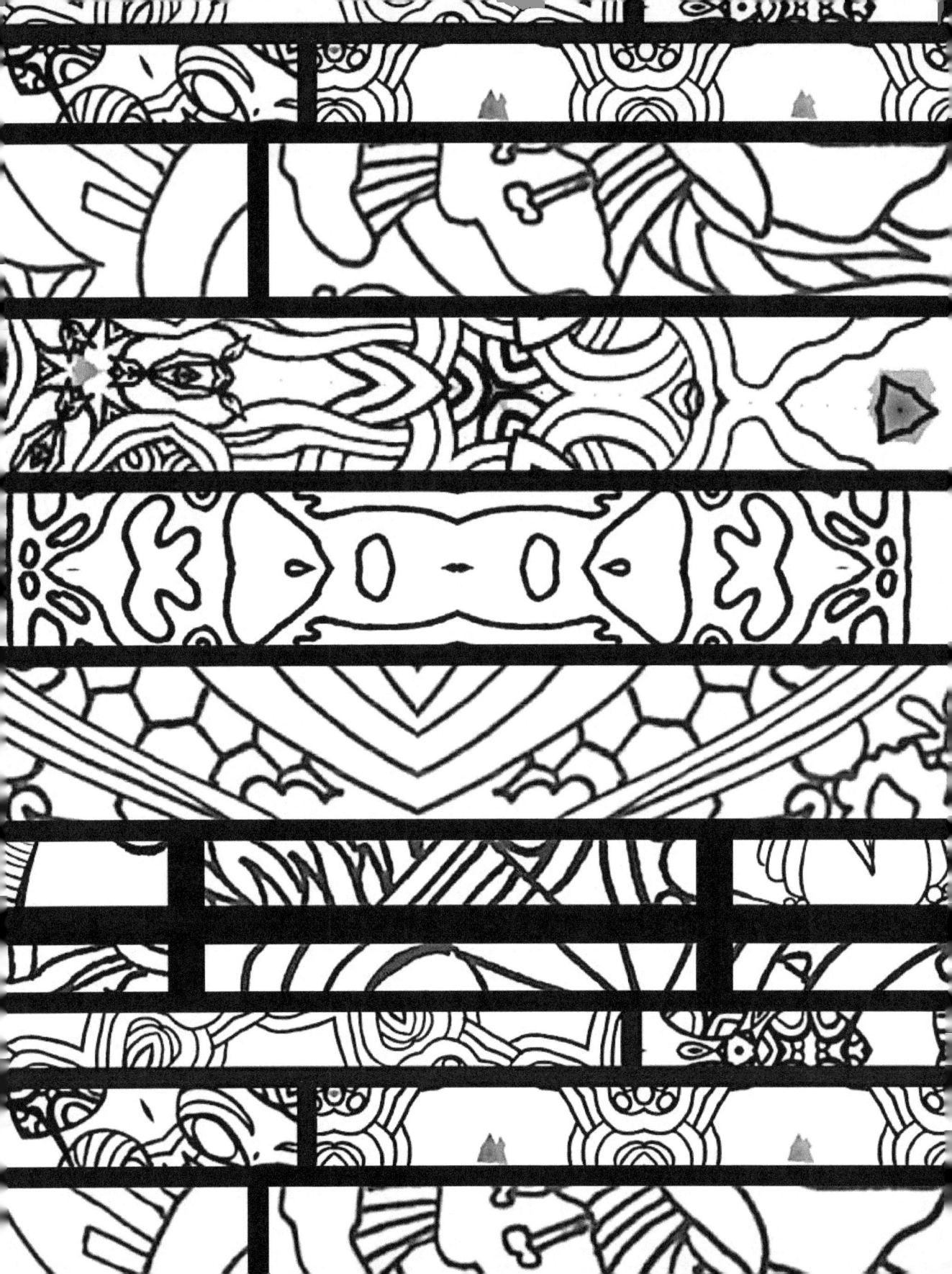

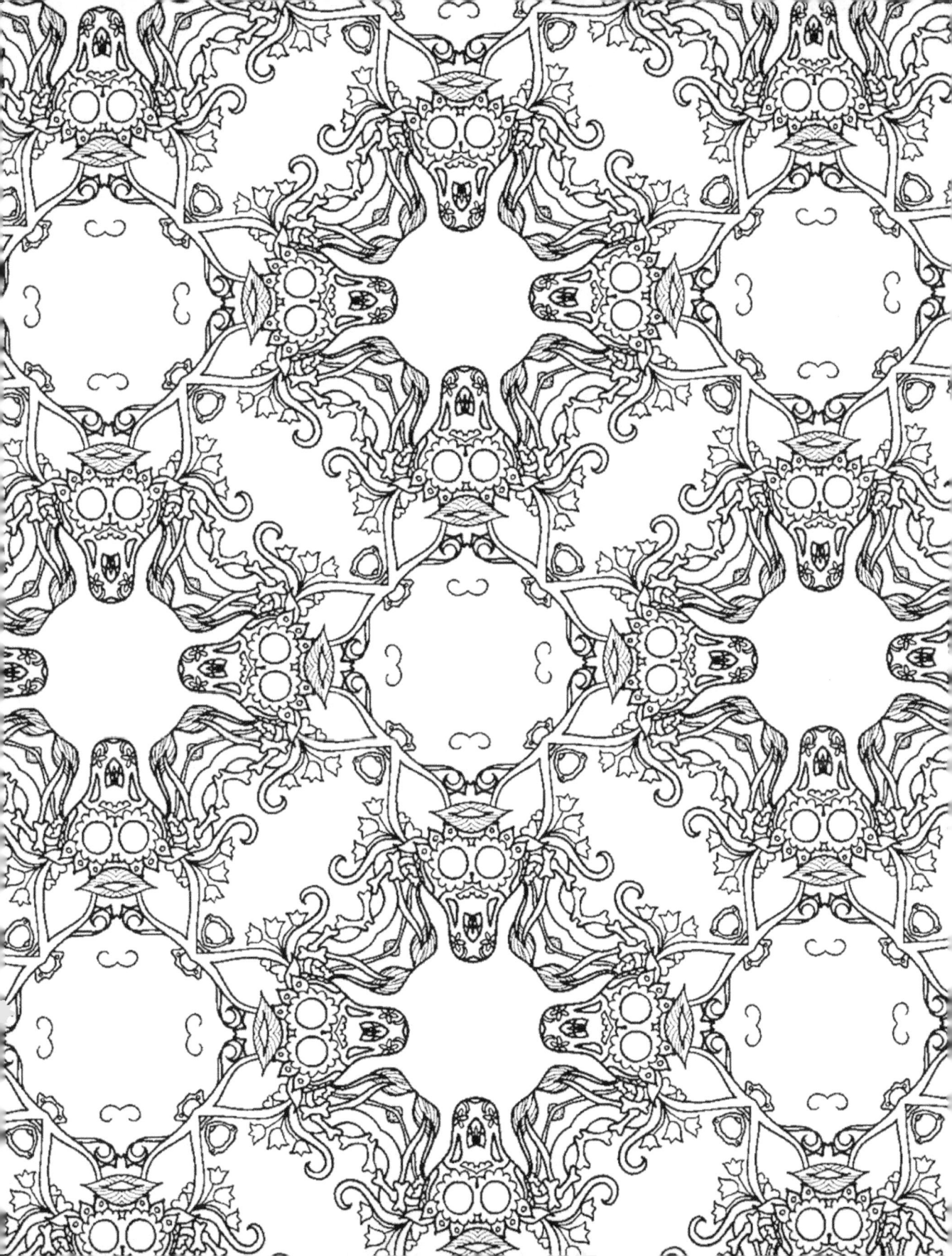

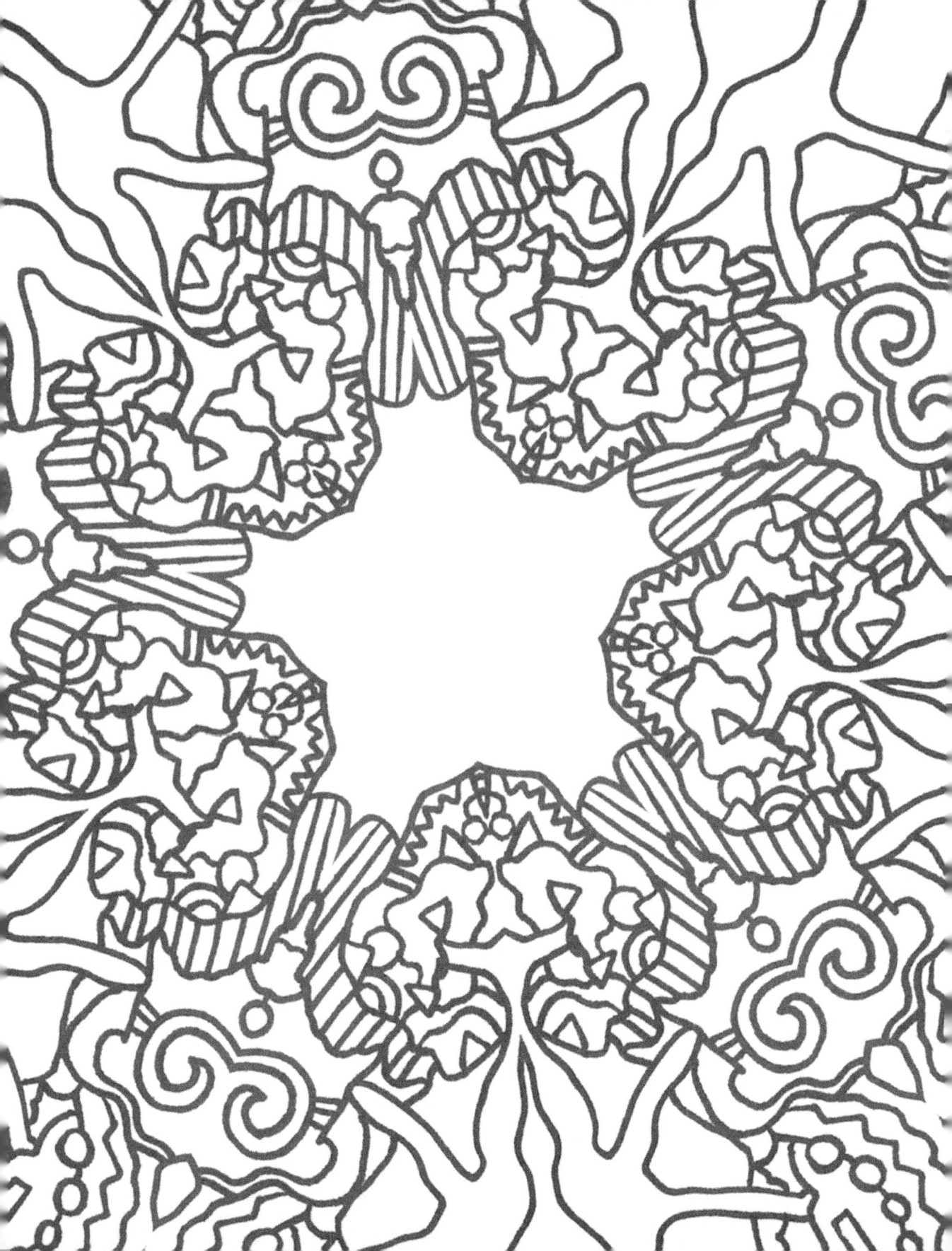

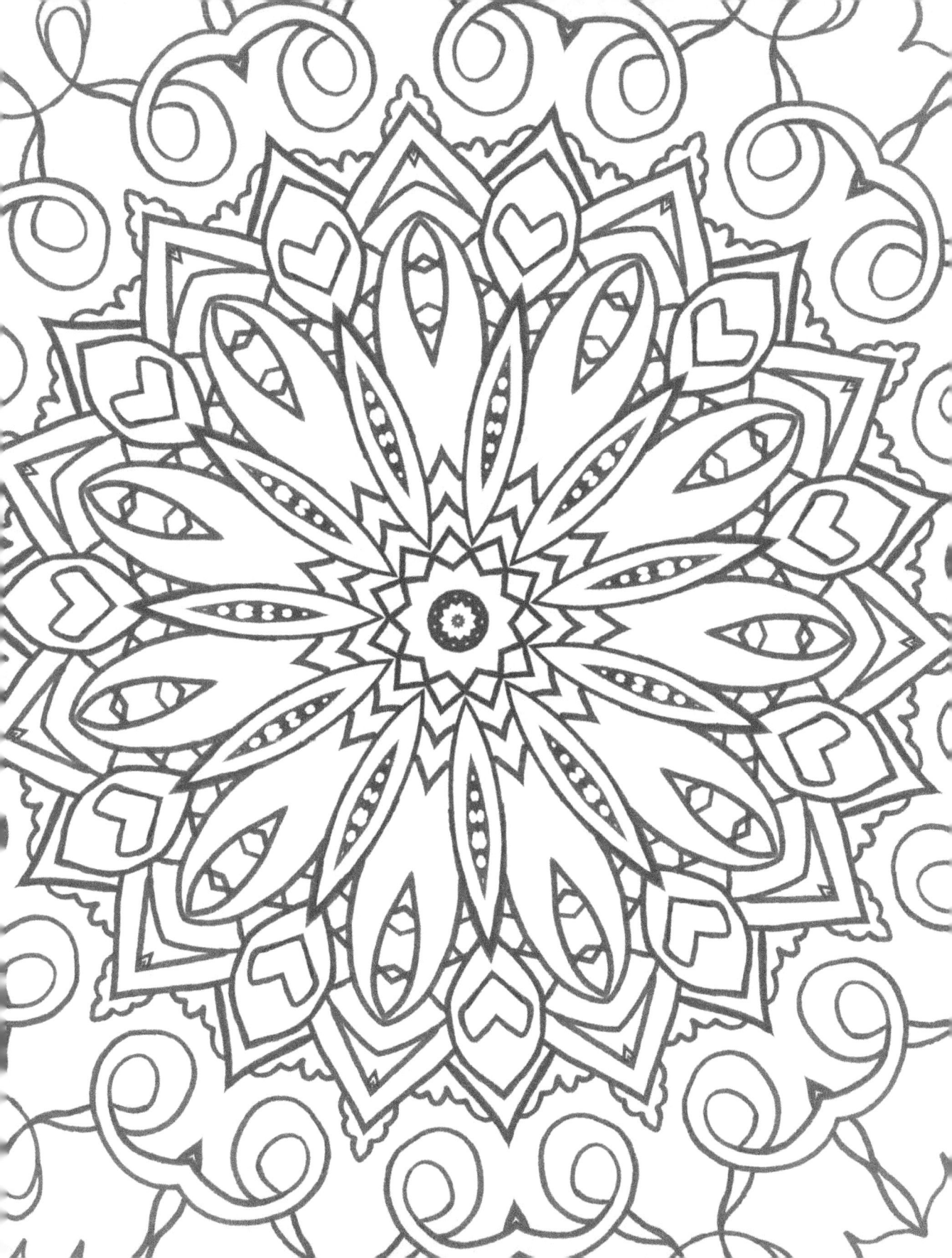

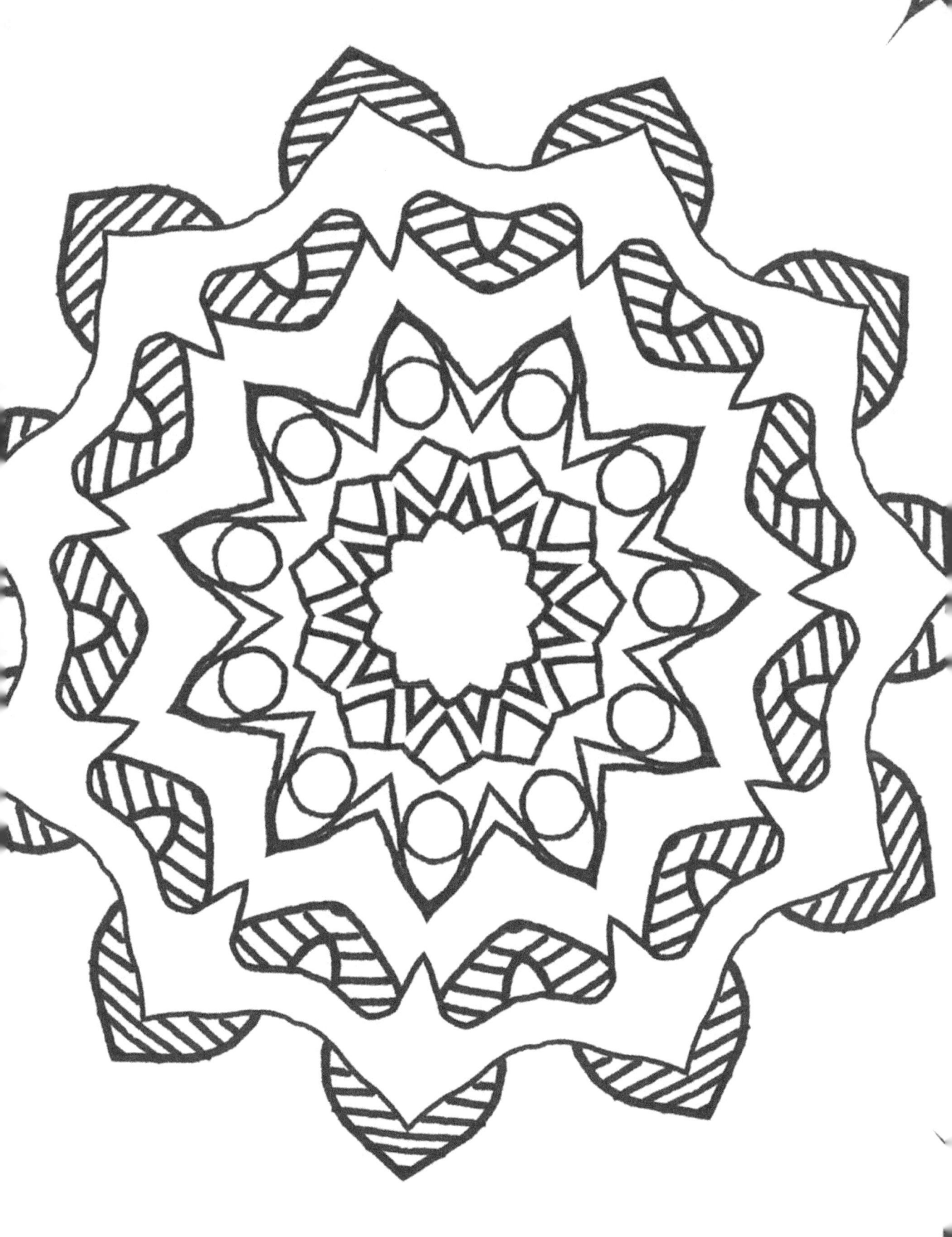

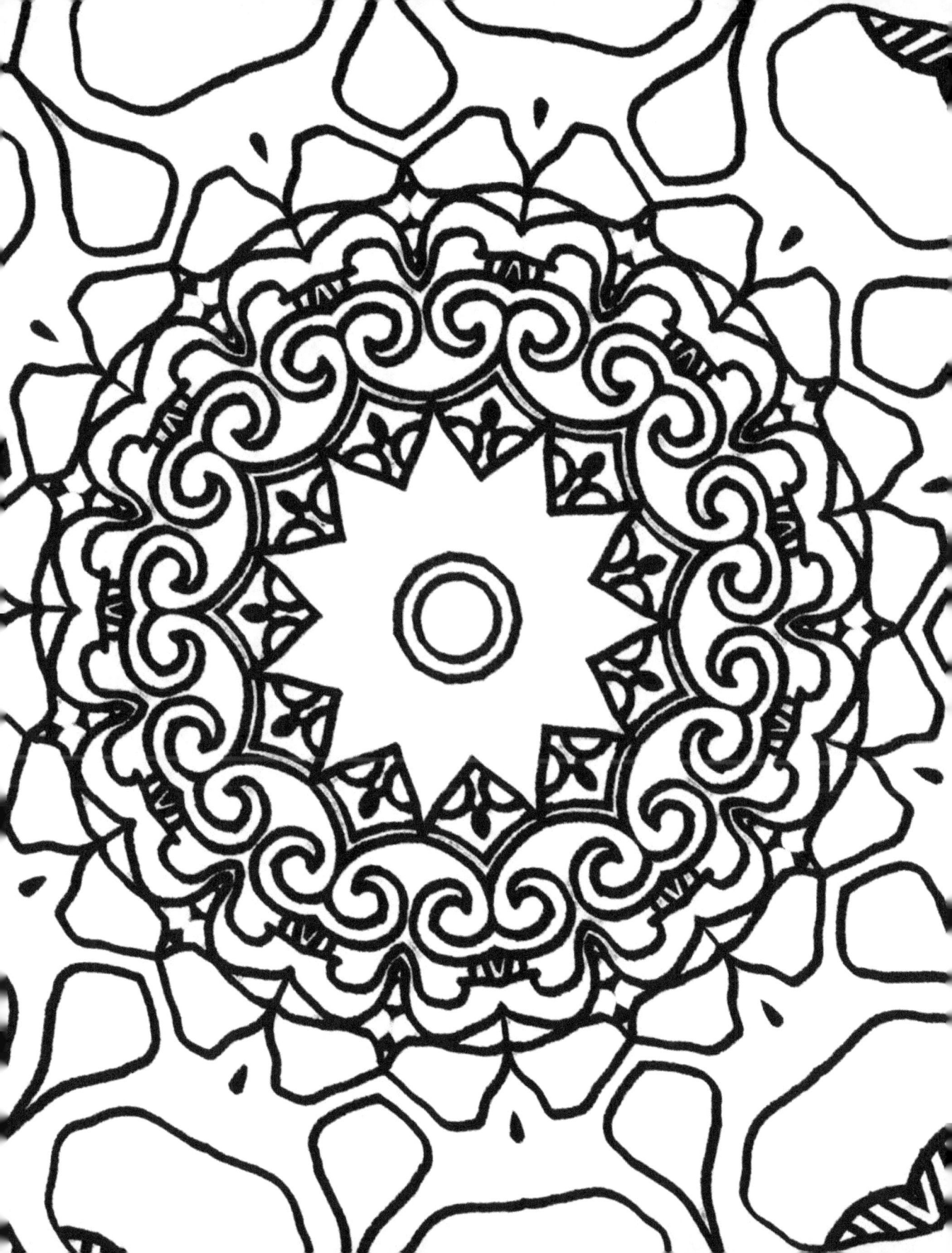

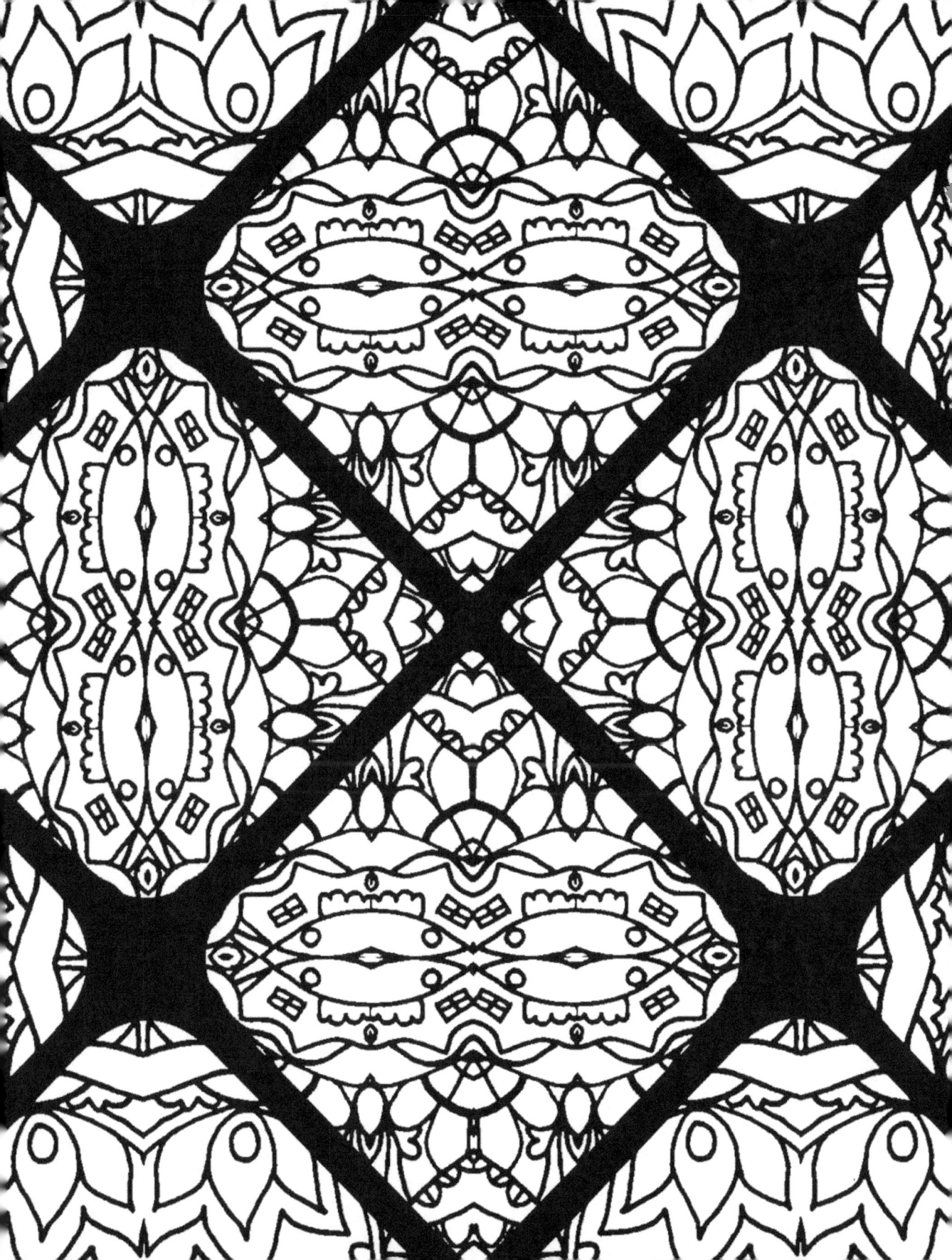

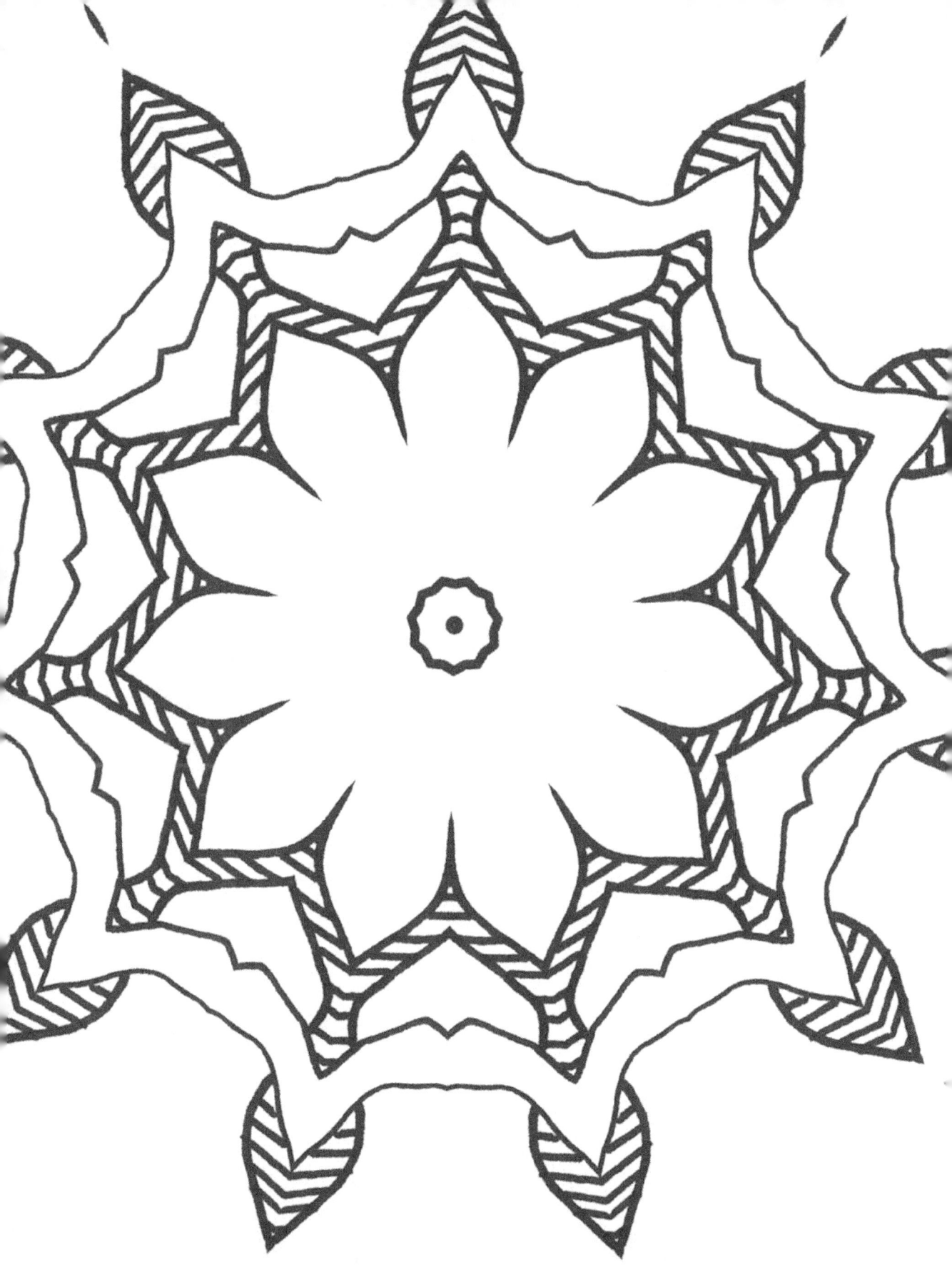

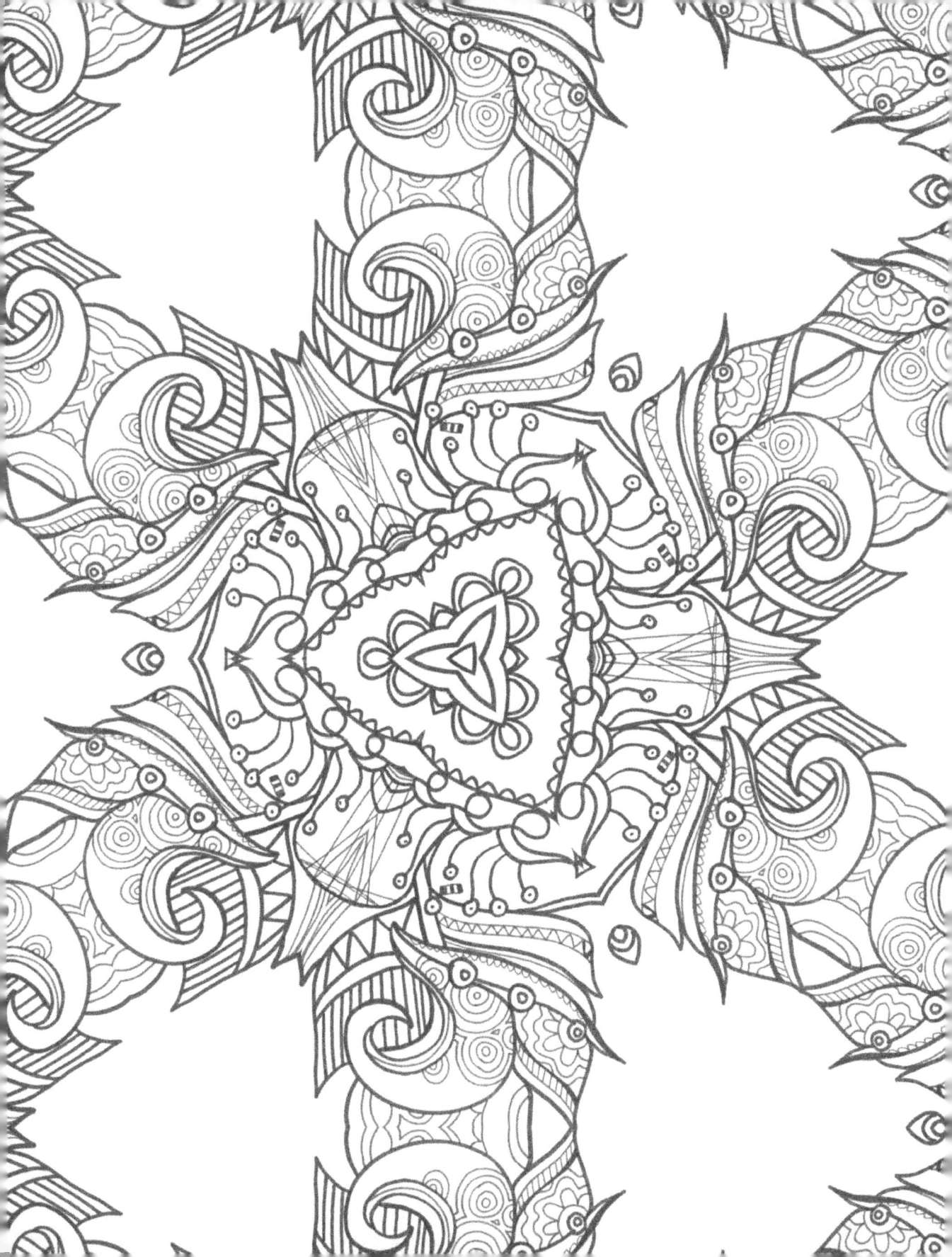

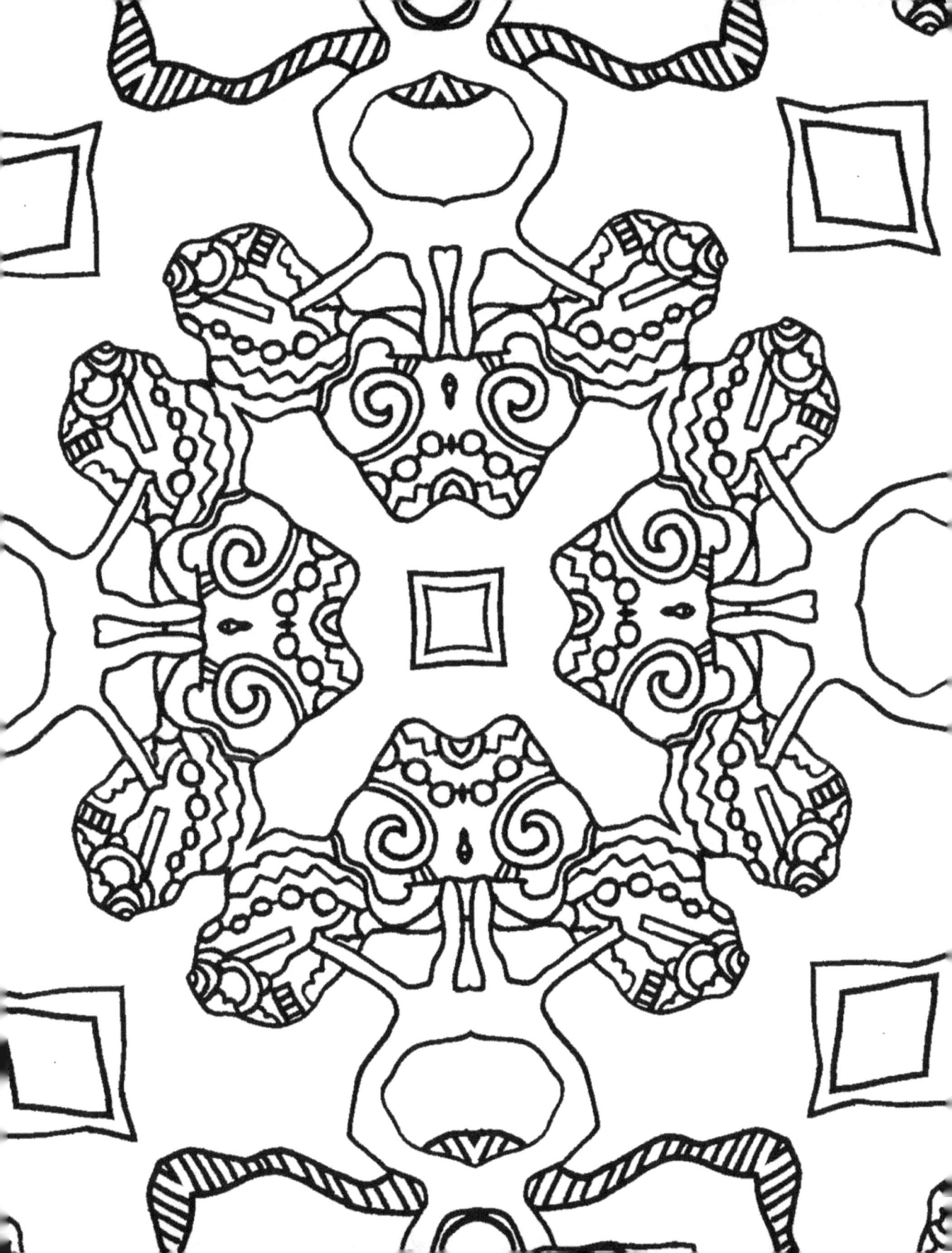

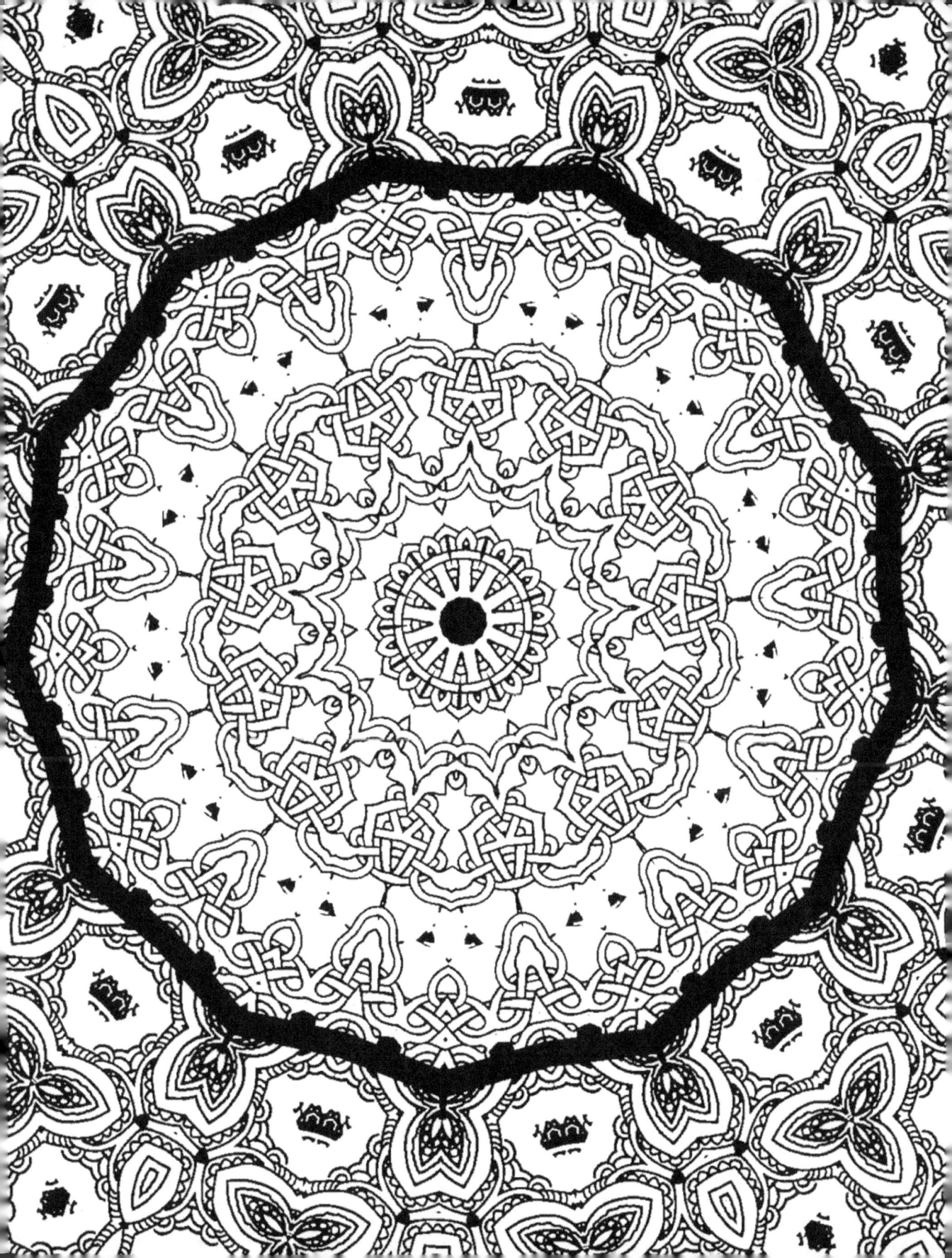

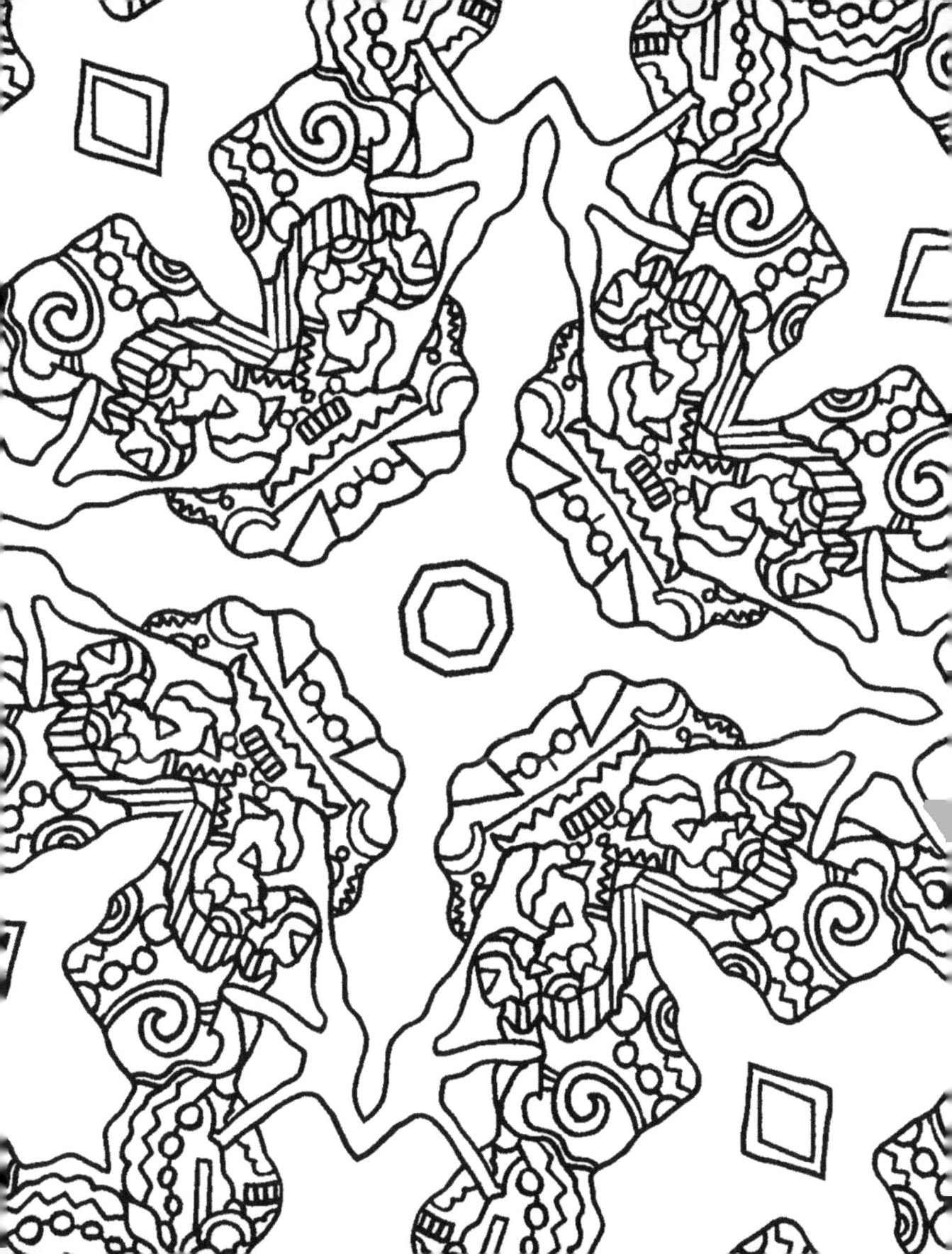

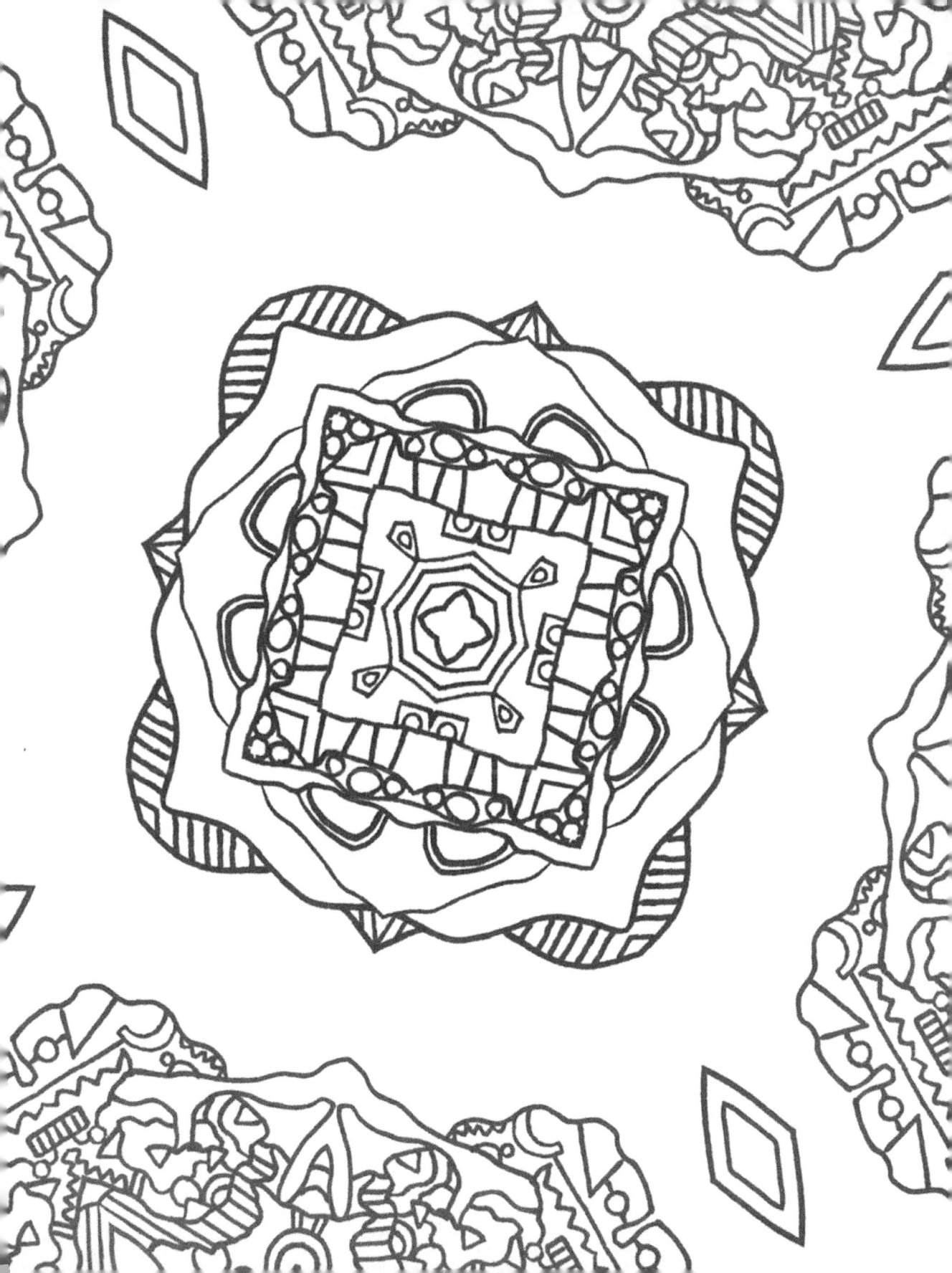

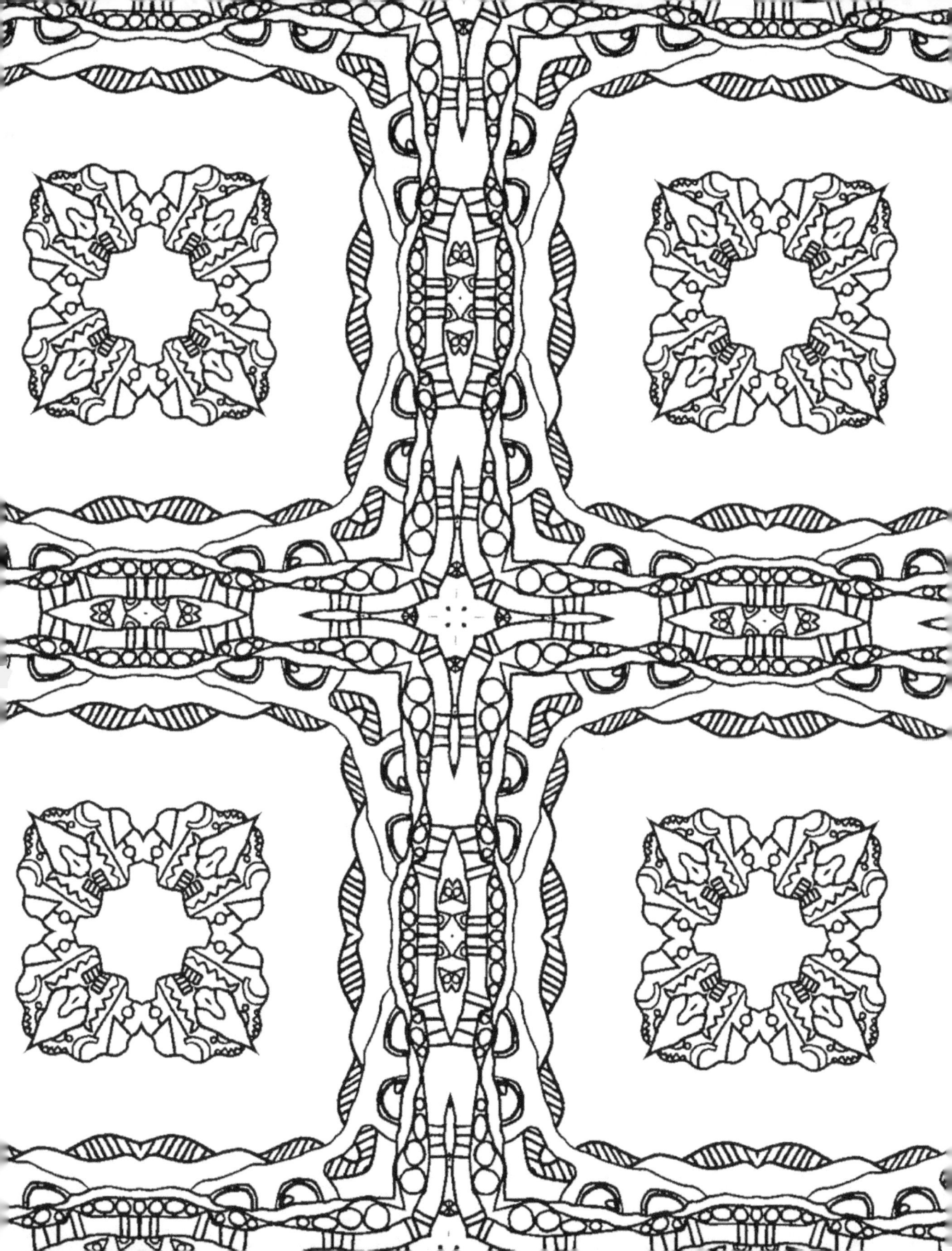

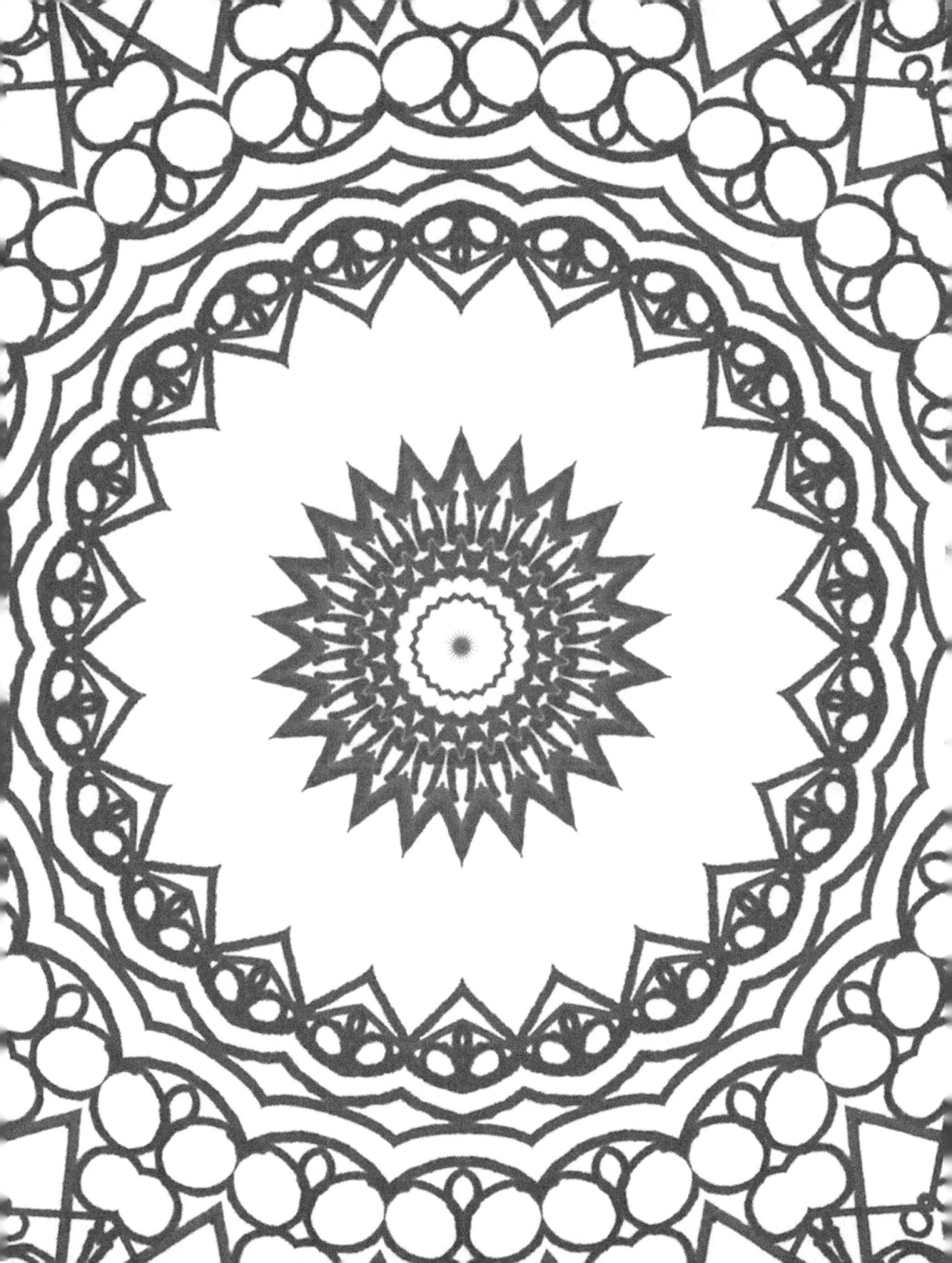

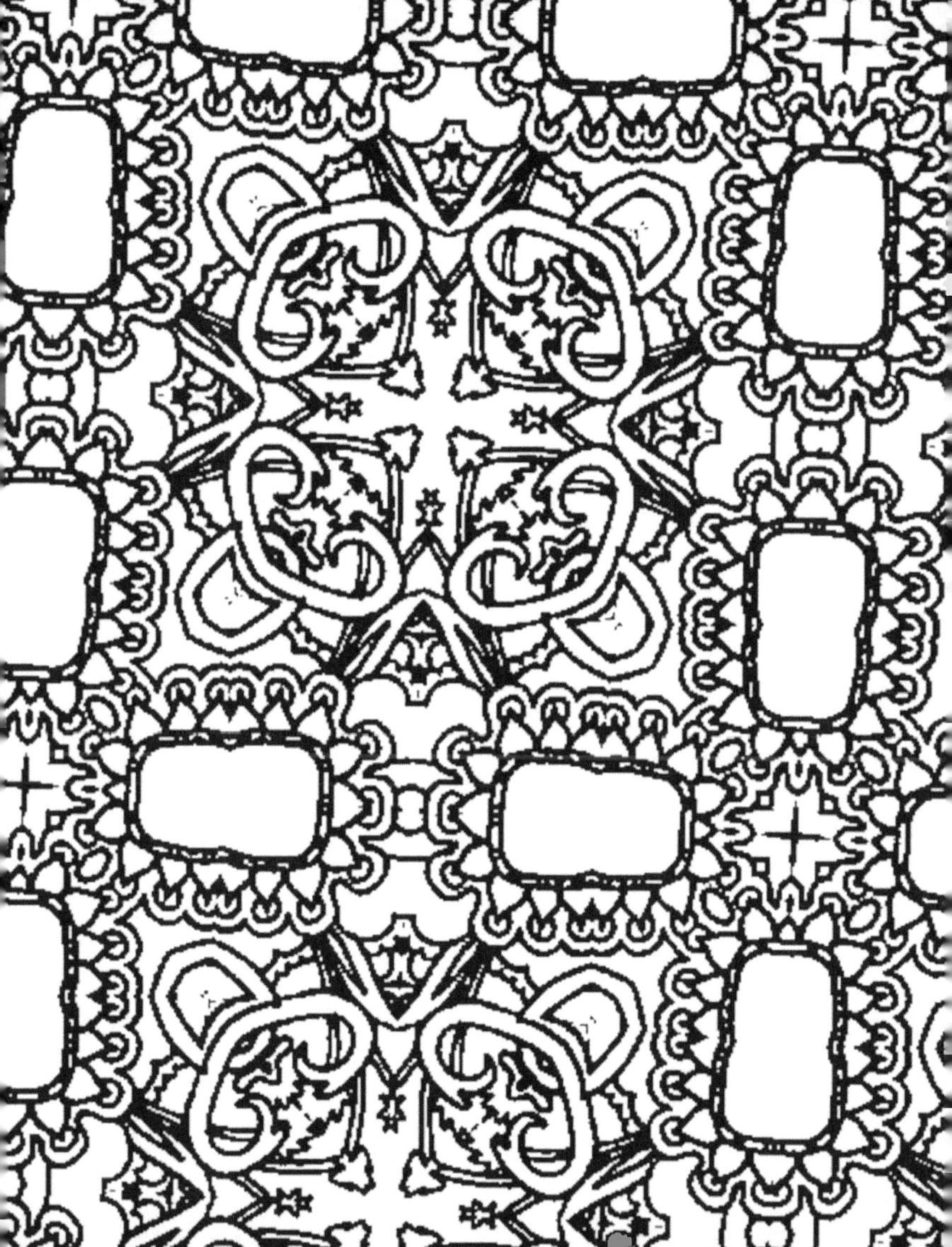

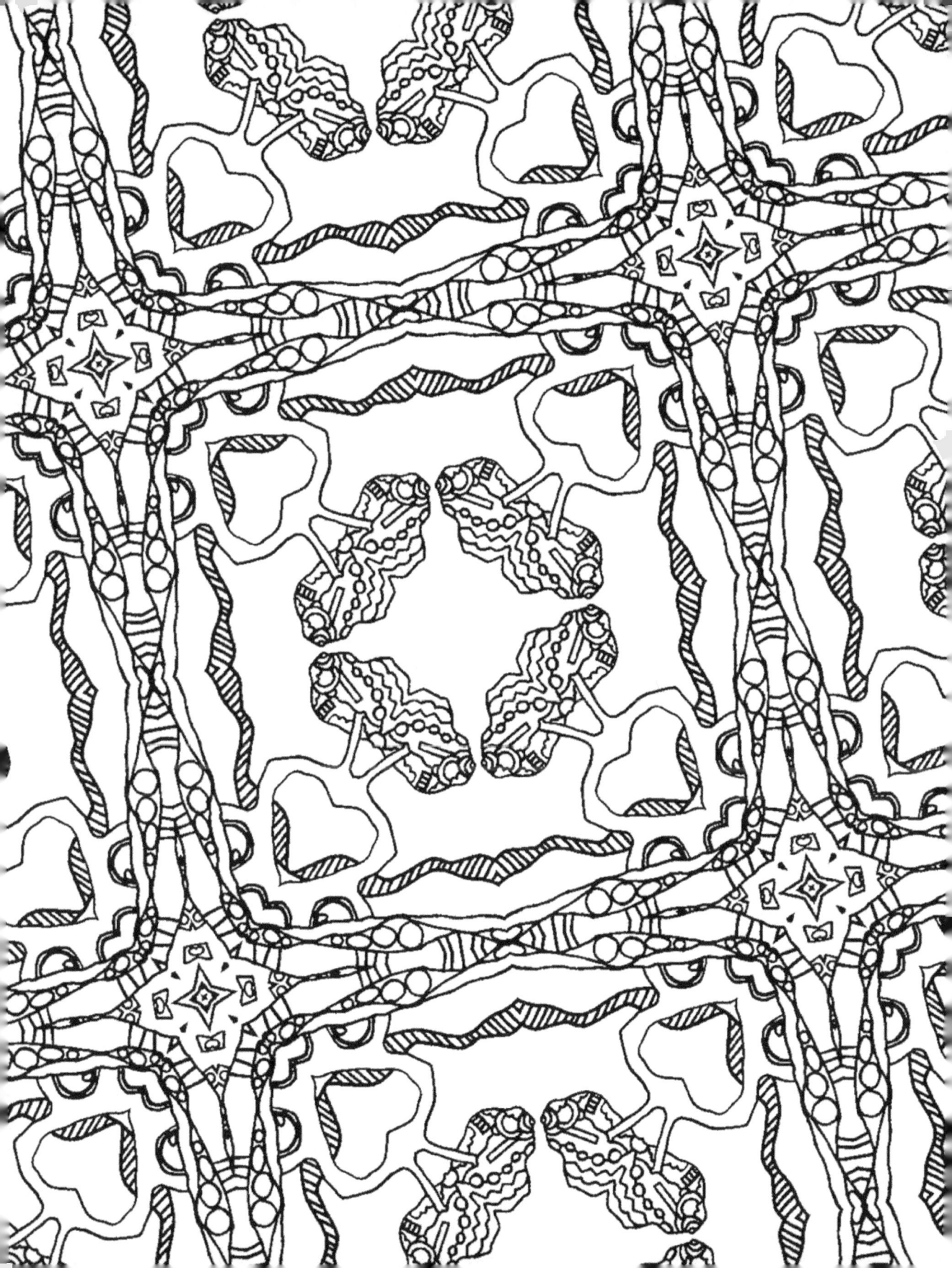

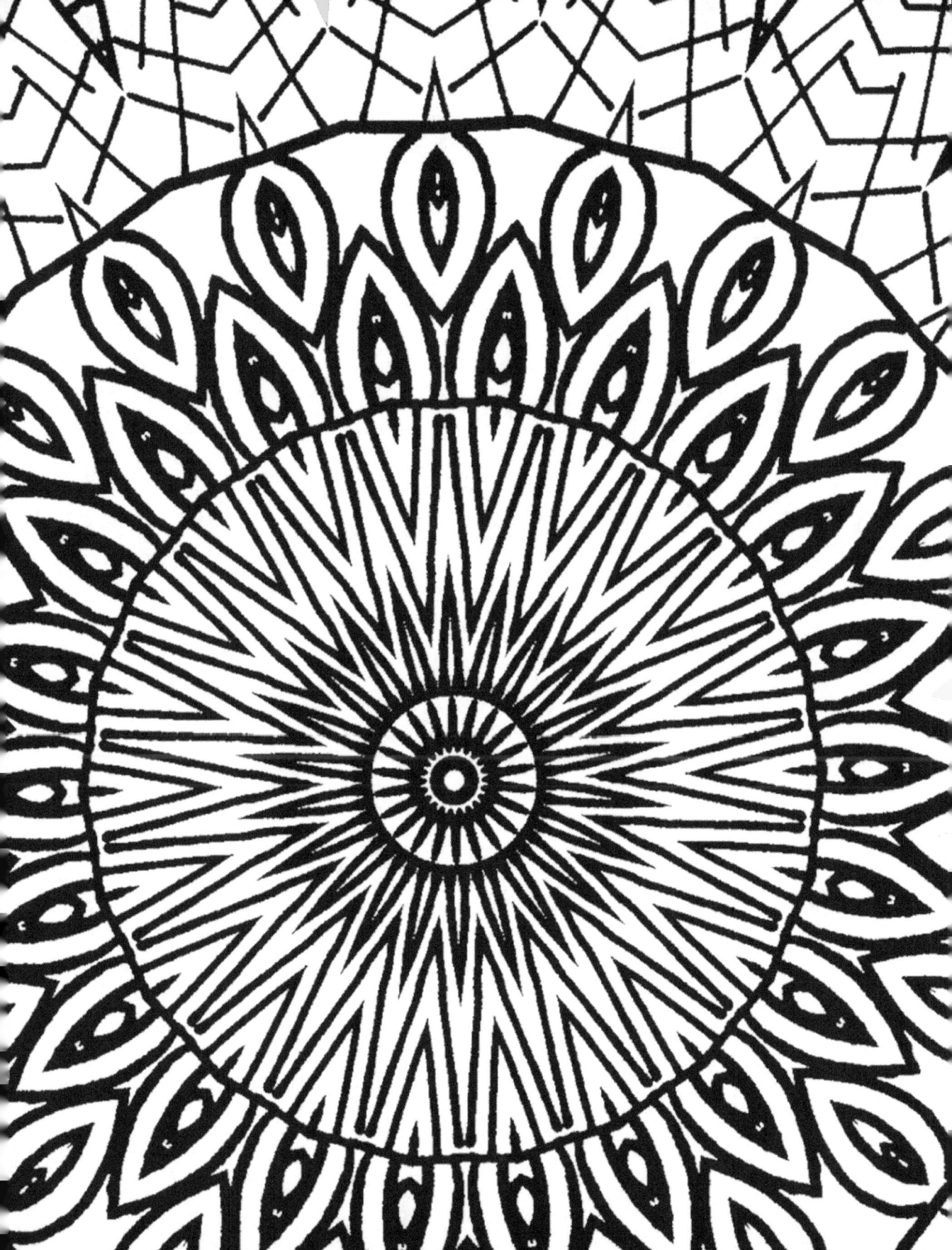

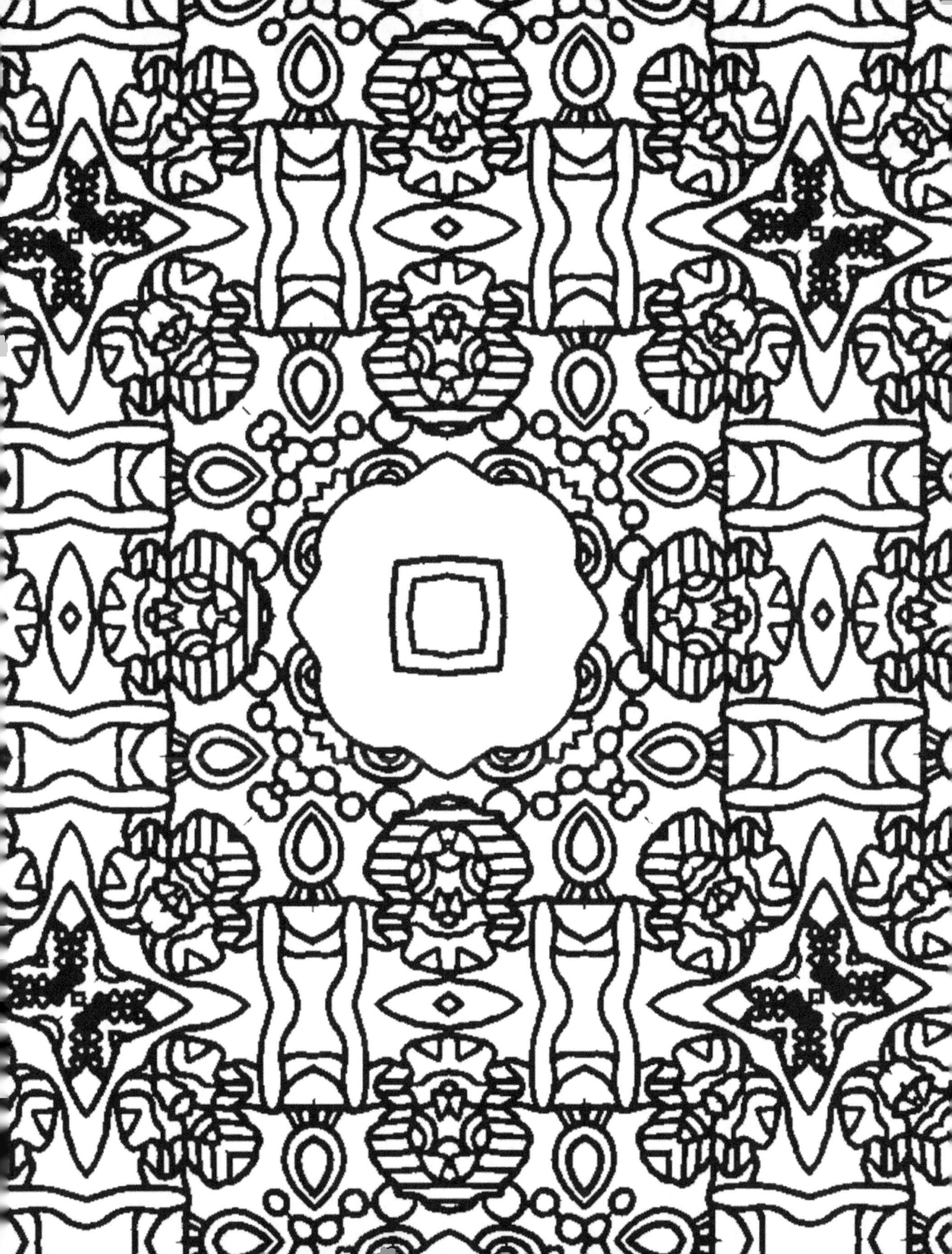

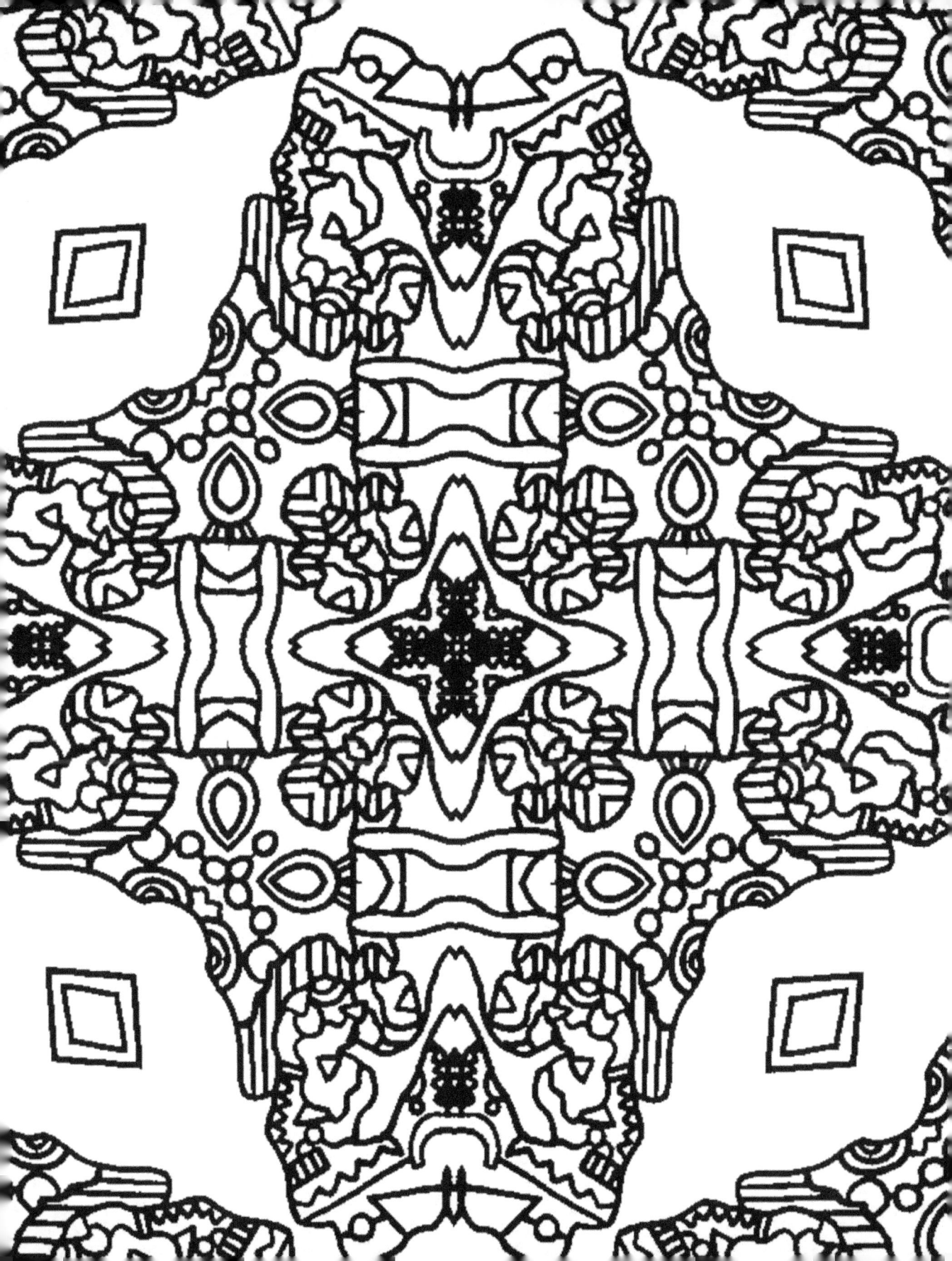

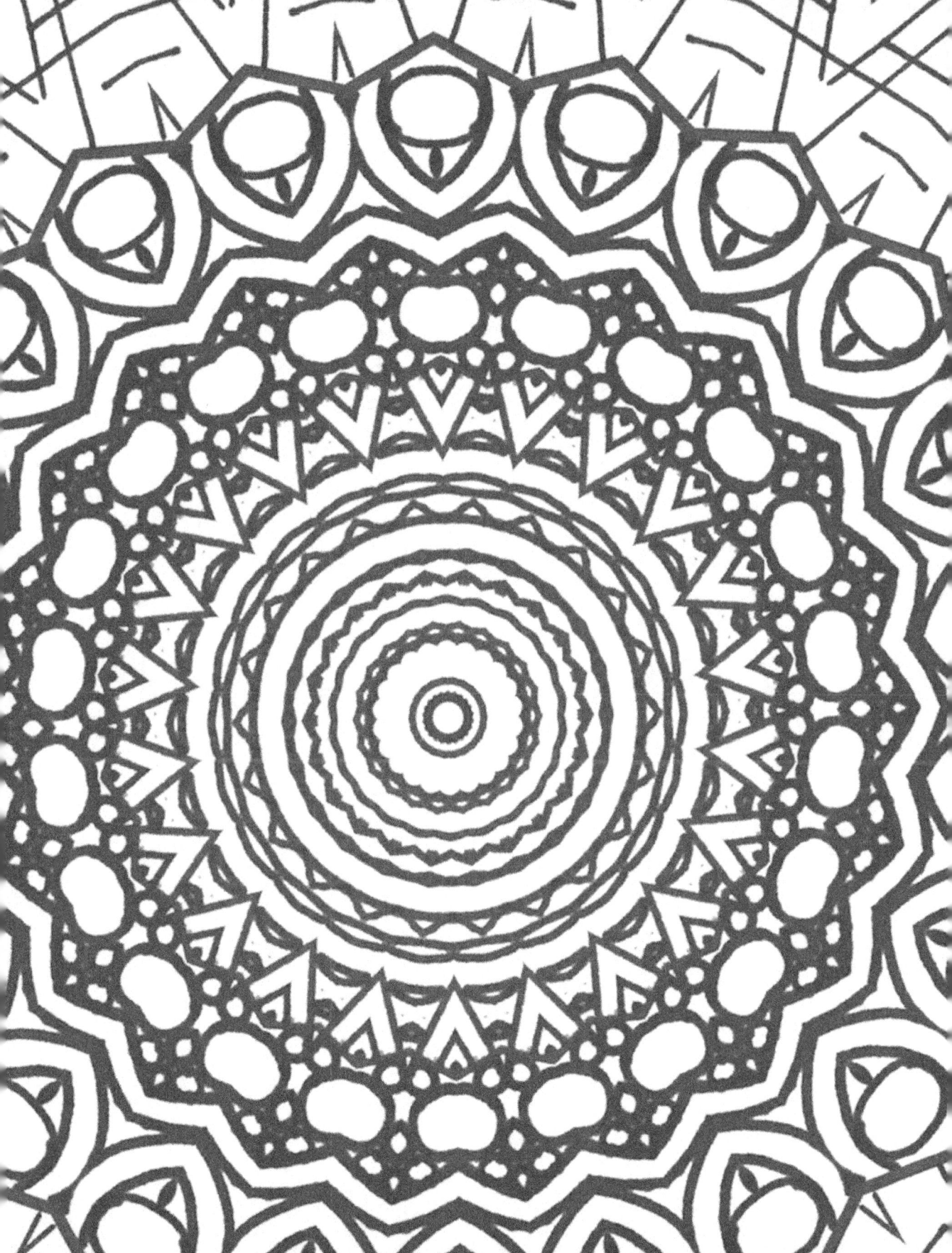

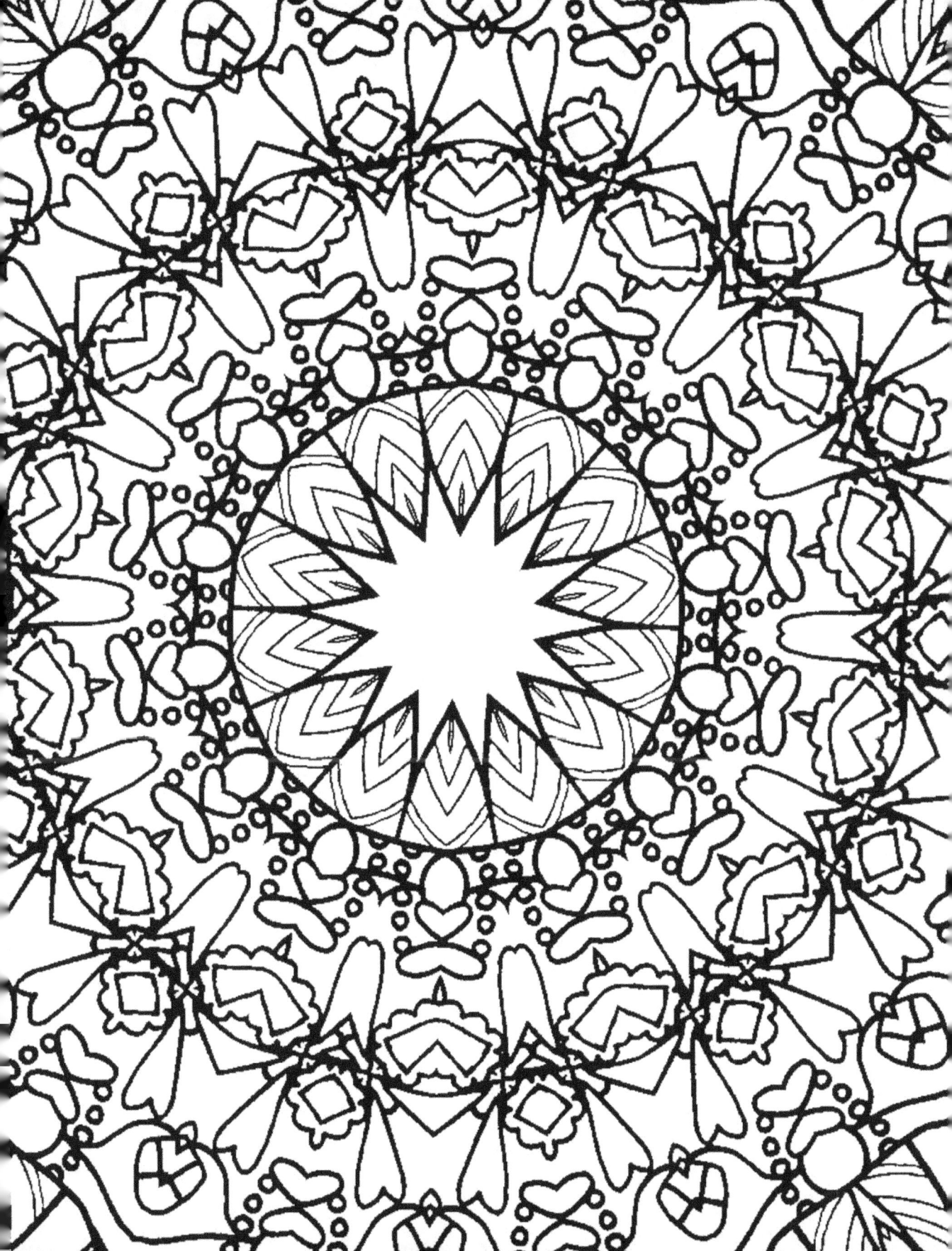

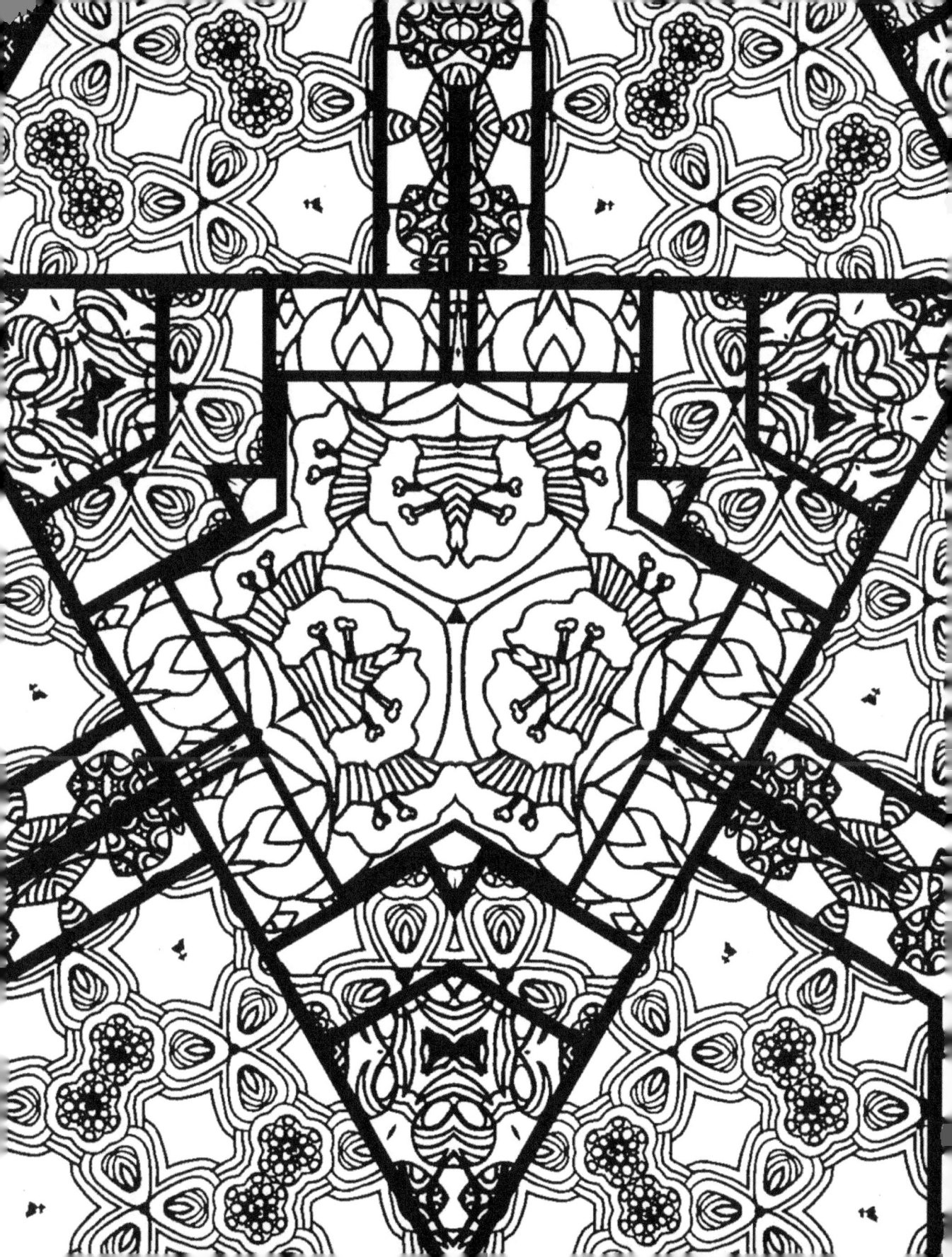

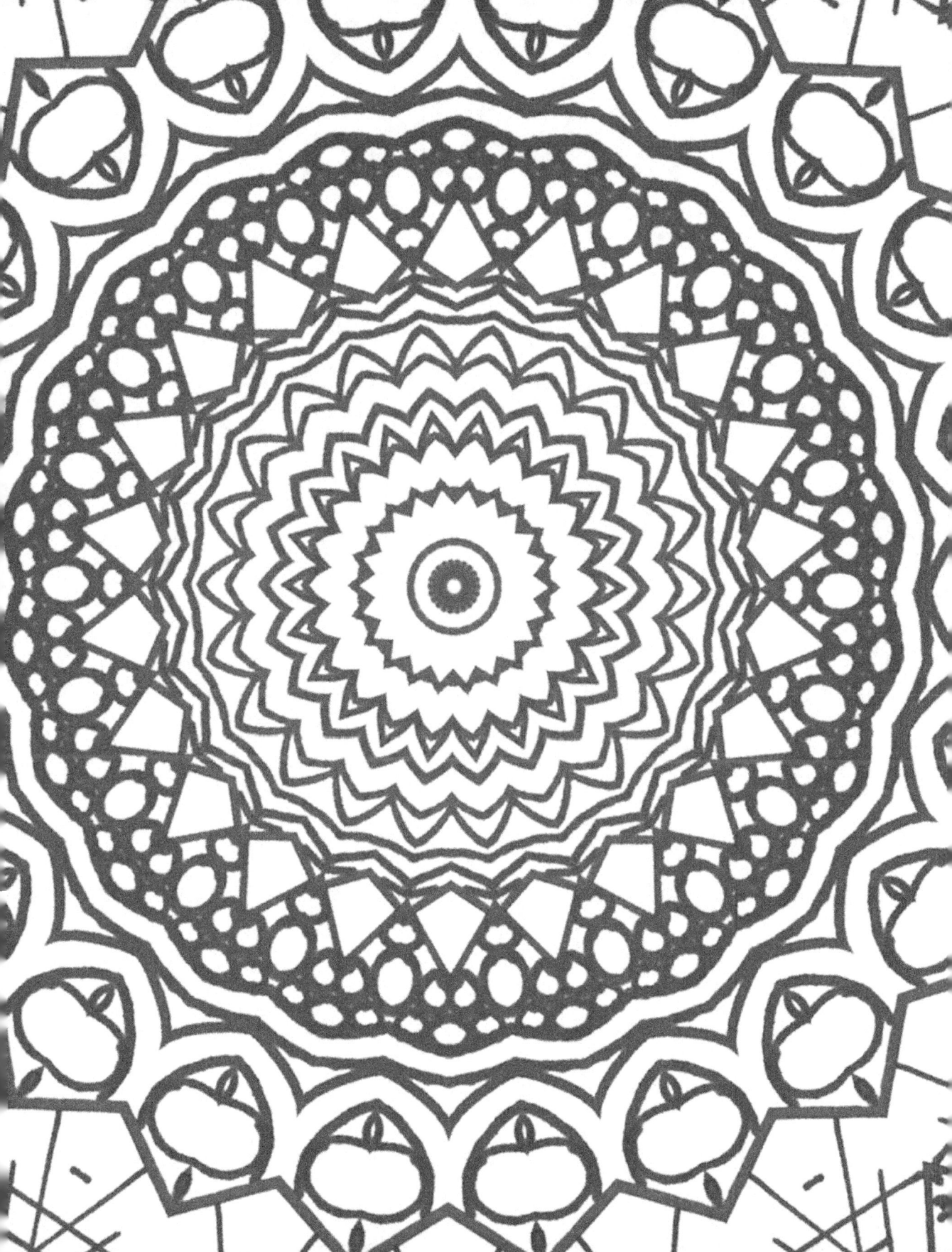

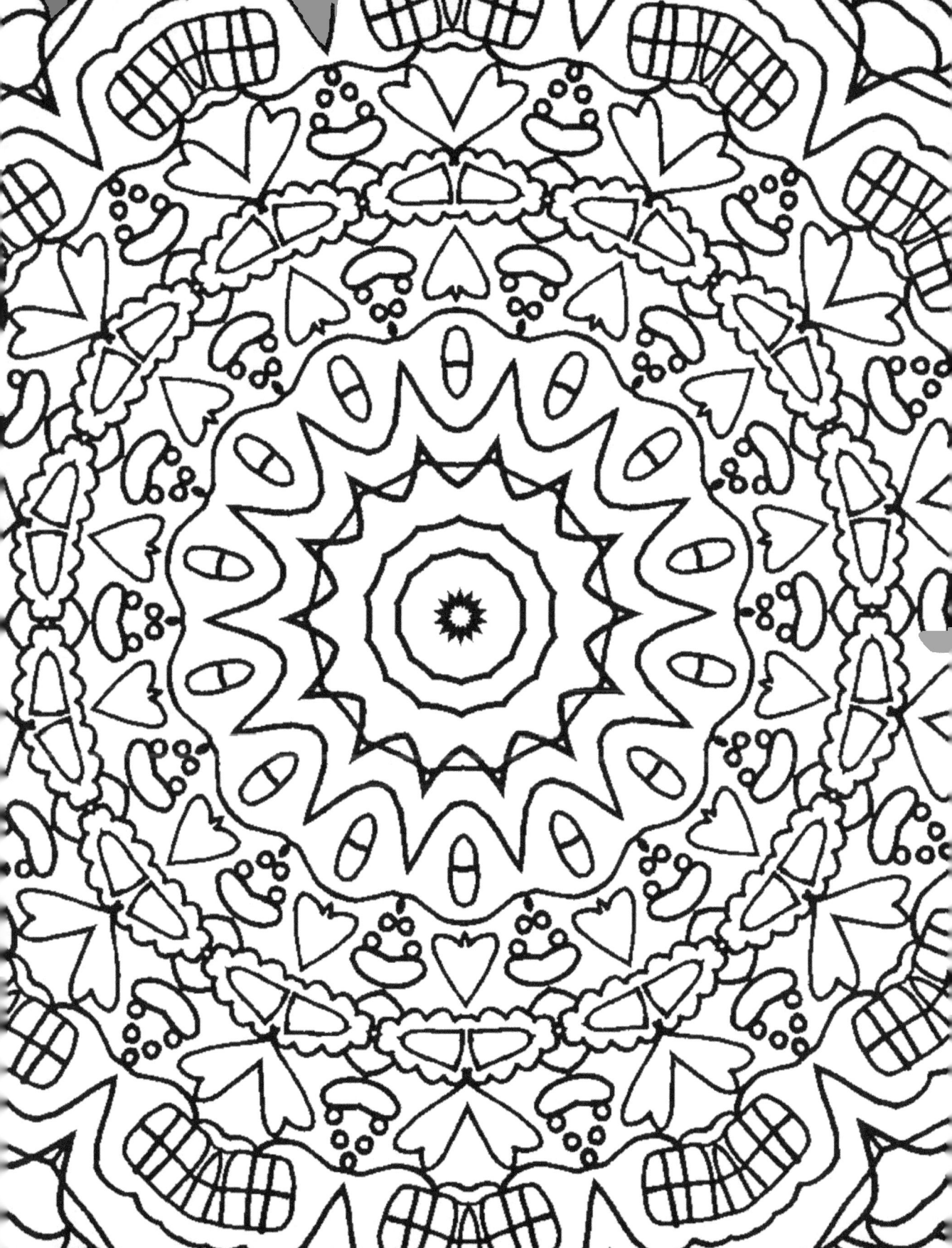

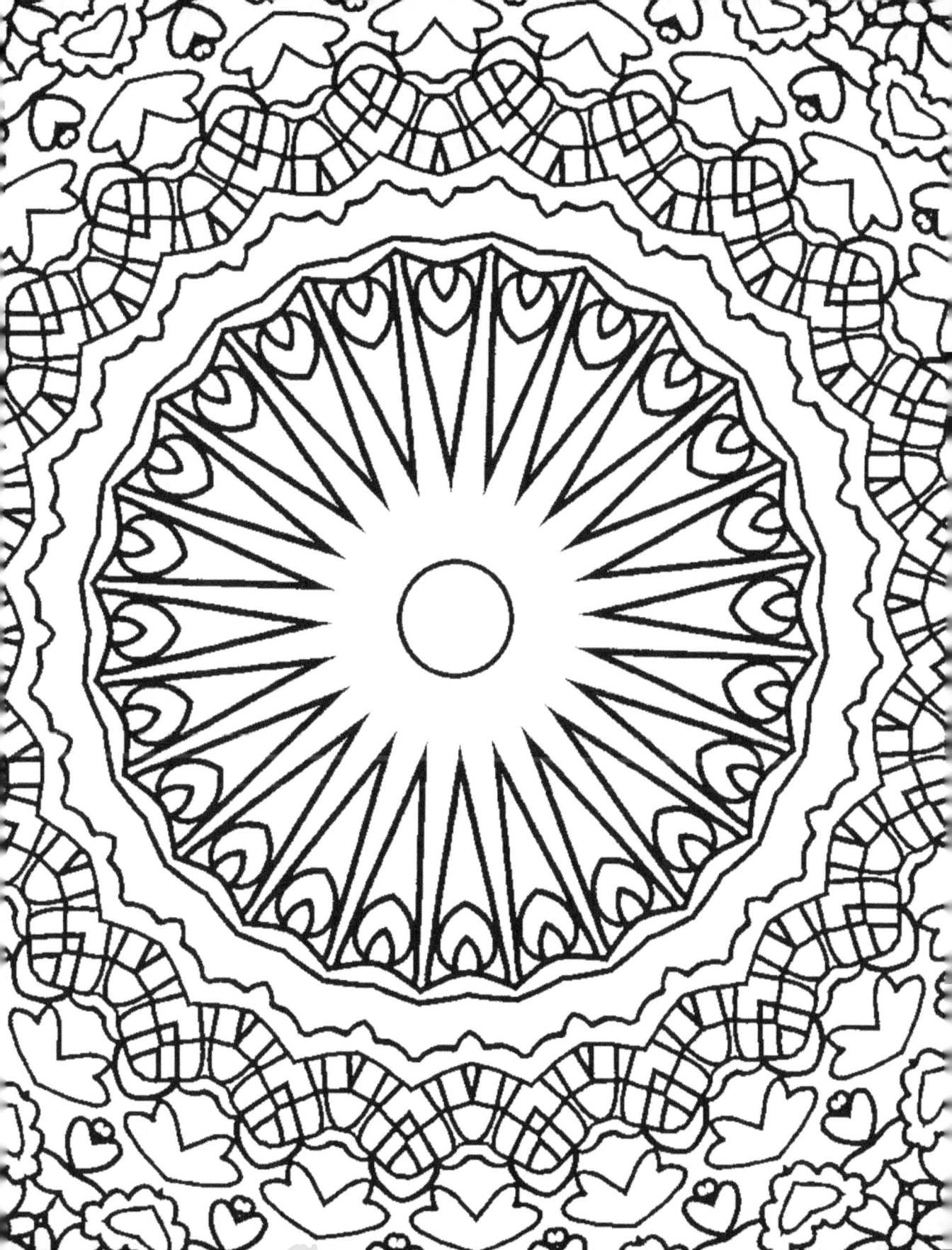

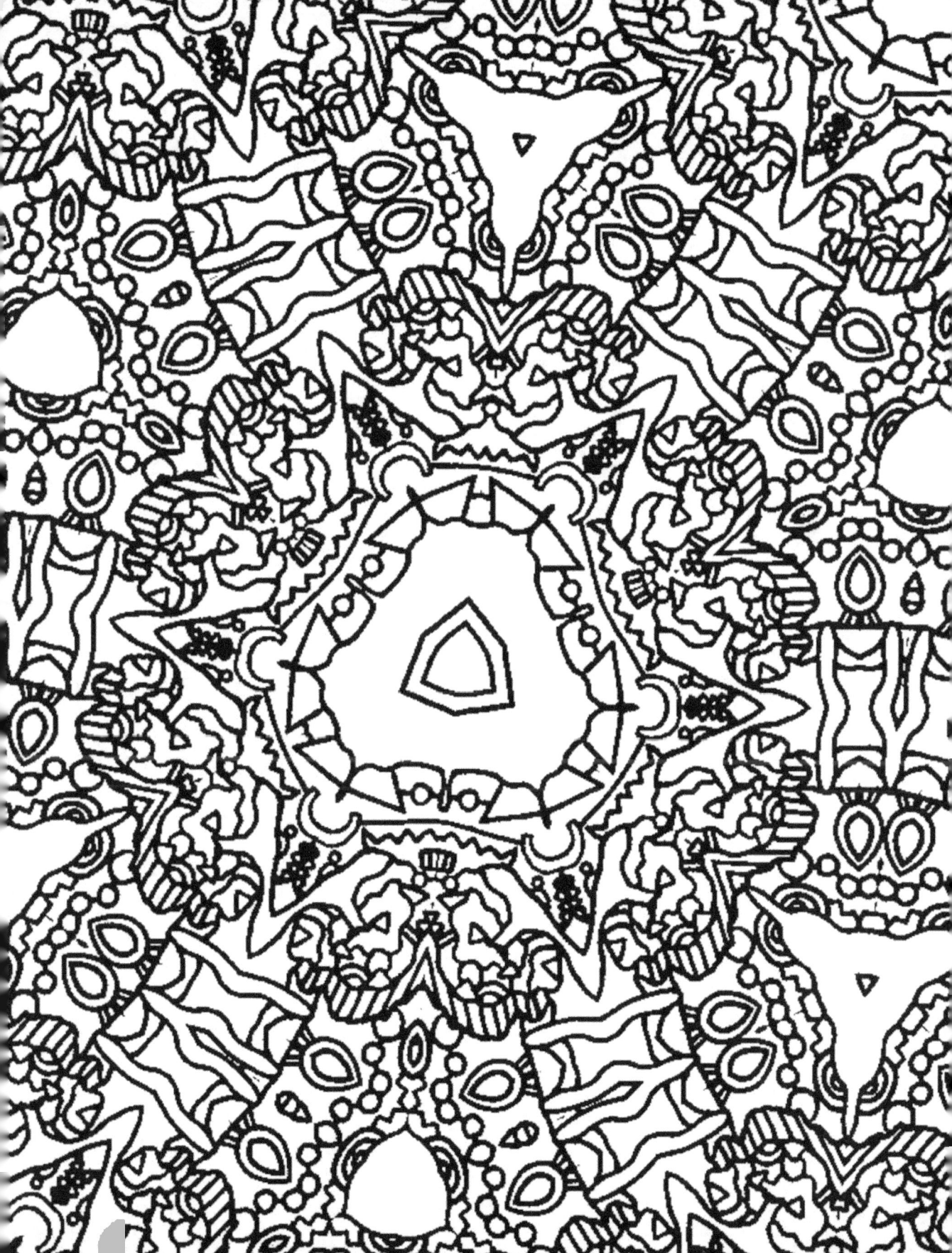

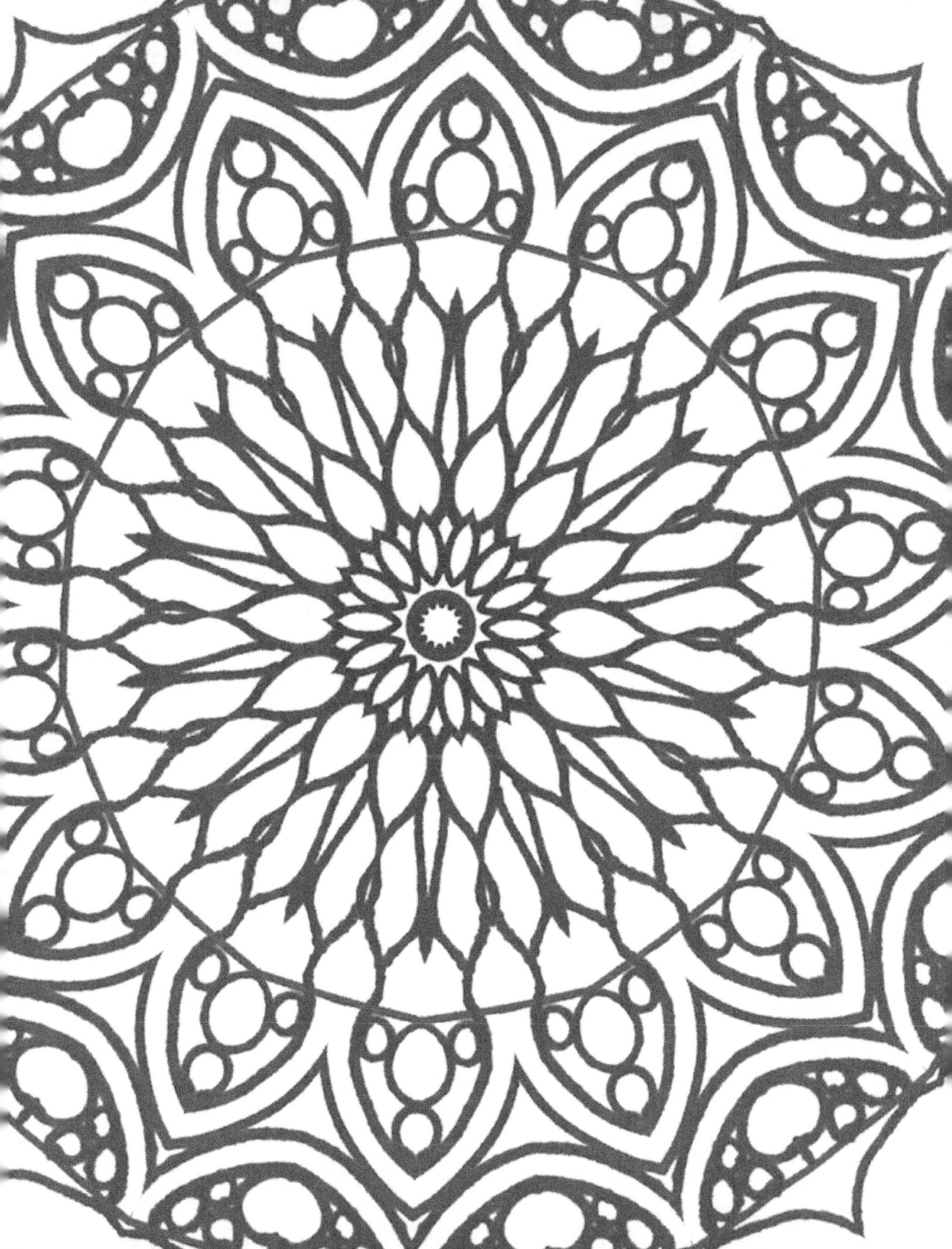

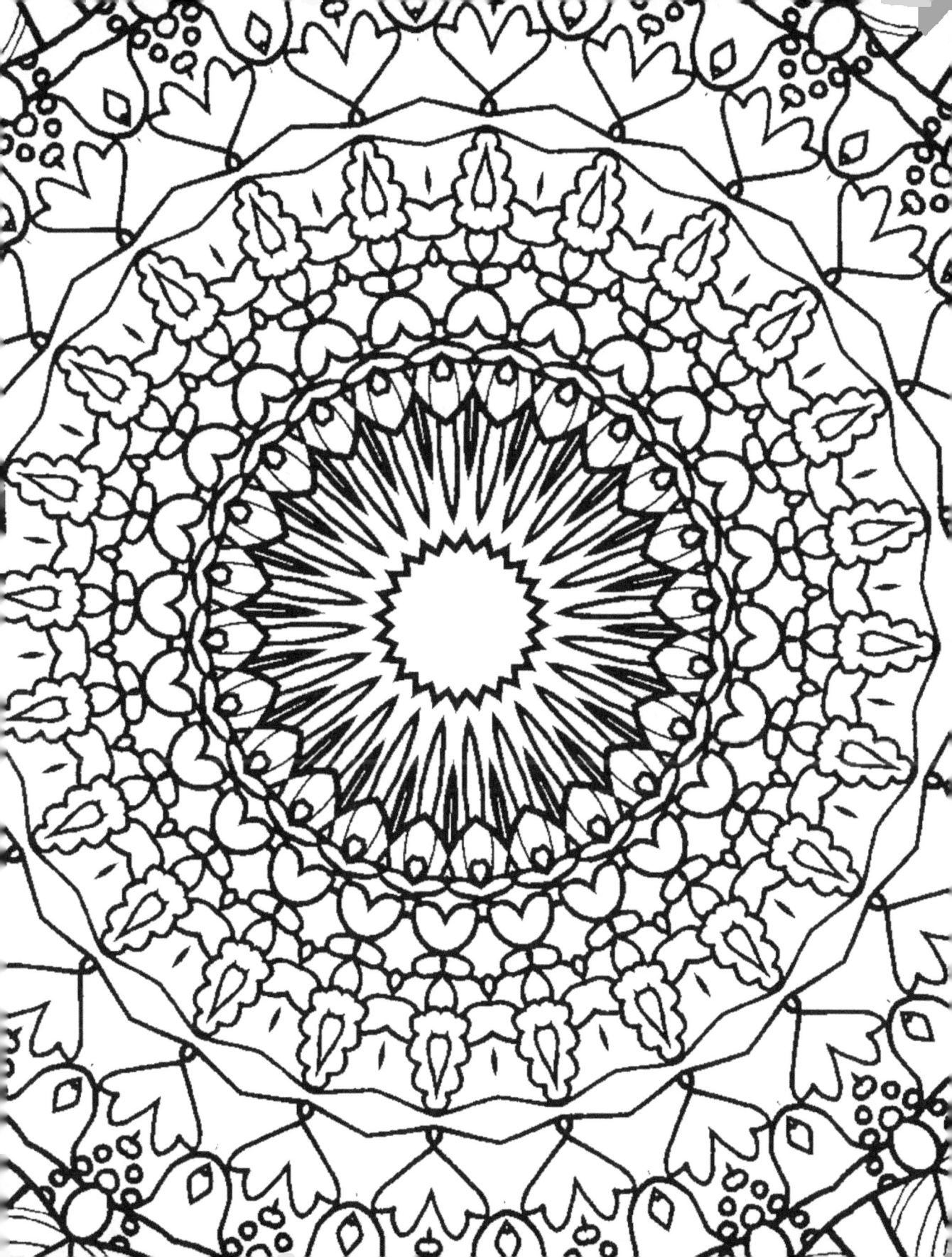

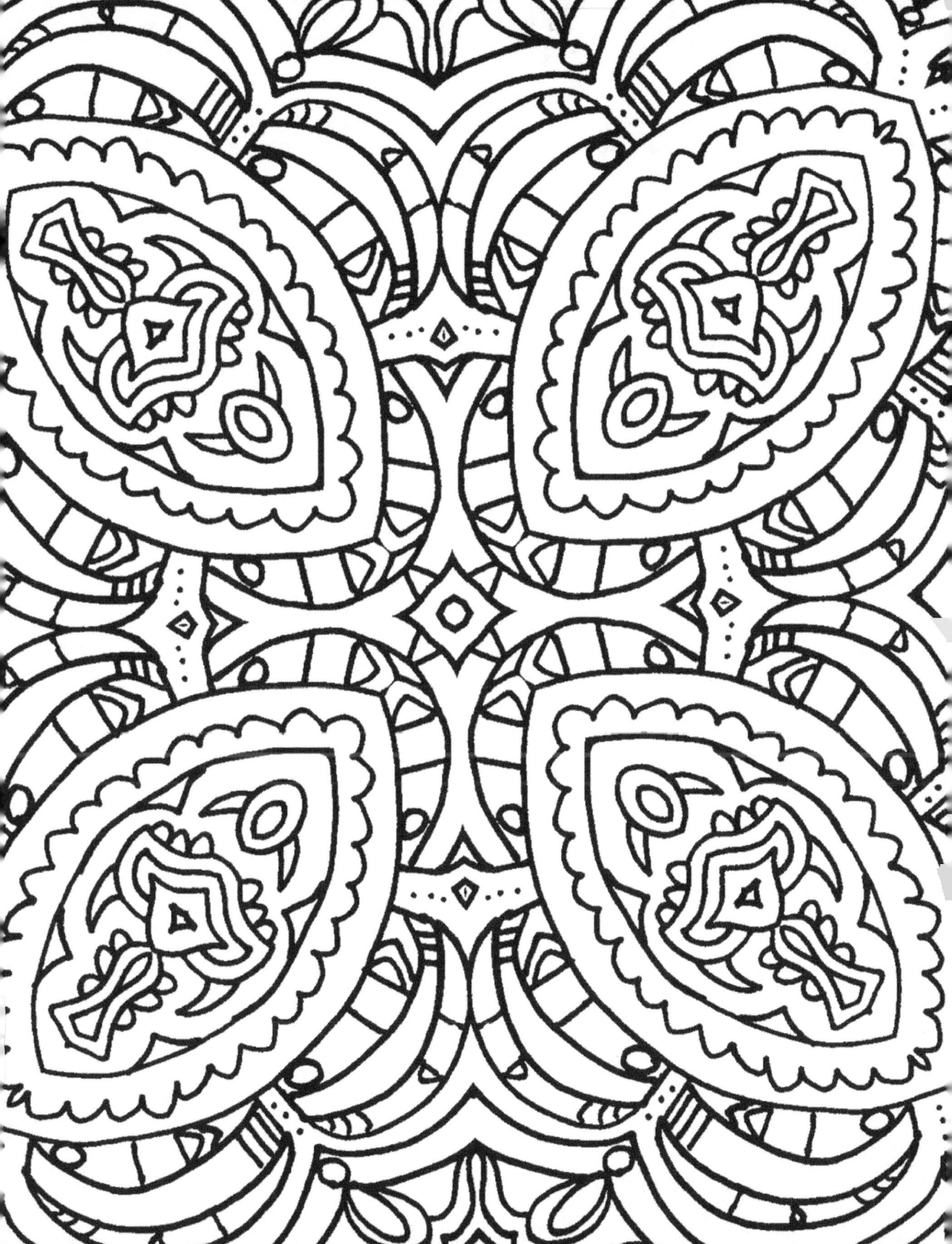

www.ingramcontent.com/pod-product-compliance
Lightning Source LLC
Chambersburg PA
CBHW080536190526
45169CB00012B/2272